THOMAS B. STODDARD is an attorney in private practice in New York City. In addition to his private practice, he currently serves as Legislative Counsel to the New York Civil Liberties Union and as Assistant Adjunct Professor of Law at New York University, where he teaches a course on the rights of gay people.

E. CARRINGTON BOGGAN is a New York City attorney who has done considerable work in the area of gay civil rights. He has served as General Counsel for Lambda Defense and Education Fund, Inc., a non-profit corporation that protects the civil rights of gay people through the legal process. He is also a past Chairperson of the American Bar Association Section on Individual Rights and Responsibilities.

MARILYN G. HAFT has worked extensively in the areas of women's rights, prisoners' rights, and sexual privacy. She has served as Director of the ACLU National Project on Sexual Privacy and has chaired subcommittees on prostitution and victimless crimes for the American Bar Association. She has also worked in the Office of the Counsel to the Vice-President of the United States and on the staff of the U.S. Mission to the United Nations.

CHARLES LISTER is an attorney in Washington, D.C. A graduate of Harvard and Oxford Universities, he has served as a Special Assistant in the Office of the Secretary of the Air Force and as law clerk to Mr. Justice Harlan of the U.S. Supreme Court. He has been as Associate Professor at the Yale Law School, and has served as a consultant on privacy and civil liberties issues to various state and federal agencies.

JOHN P. RUPP is a graduate of the Yale Law School, and is a member of the bars of the District of Columbia and Maine. He has previously worked in the Office of the Solicitor General of the United States, and is presently an attorney in Washington, D.C.

Other Bantam Books in the series
Ask your bookseller for the titles you have missed

QUANTITY PURCHASES

Companies, professional groups, churches, clubs and other organizations may qualify for special terms when ordering 24 or more copies of this title. For information, contact the Direct Response Department, Bantam Books, 666 Fifth Avenue, New York, N.Y. 10103. Phone (212) 765-6500.

AN AMERICAN CIVIL LIBERTIES UNION HANDBOOK

THE RIGHTS OF GAY PEOPLE

Thomas B. Stoddard
E. Carrington Boggan
Marilyn G. Haft
Charles Lister
John P. Rupp

The Revised Edition of
The Basic ACLU Guide to
A Gay Person's Rights

General Editor of this series:
Norman Dorsen, *President, ACLU.*

BANTAM BOOKS
TORONTO · NEW YORK · LONDON · SYDNEY

THE RIGHTS OF GAY PEOPLE
A Bantam Book

PRINTING HISTORY
Bantam revised edition / April 1983

ISBN 0-553-23136-7

Published simultaneously in the United States and Canada

Bantam Books are published by Bantam Books, Inc. Its trade-
mark, consisting of the words "Bantam Books" and the portrayal
of a rooster, is Registered in U.S. Patent and Trademark
Office and in other countries. Marca Registrada. Bantam
Books, Inc., 666 Fifth Avenue, New York, New York 10103.

PRINTED IN THE UNITED STATES OF AMERICA

O   0 9 8 7 6 5 4 3 2 1

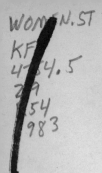

Contents

Preface

This guide sets forth your rights under the present law, and offers suggestions on how they can be protected. It is one of a continuing series of handbooks published in cooperation with the American Civil Liberties Union (ACLU).

Surrounding these publications is the hope that Americans, informed of their rights, will be encouraged to exercise them. Through their exercise, rights are given life. If they are rarely used, they may be forgotten and violations may become routine.

This guide offers no assurances that your rights will be respected. The laws may change and, in some of the subjects covered in these pages, they change quite rapidly. An effort has been made to note those parts of the law where movement is taking place, but it is not always possible to predict accurately when the law *will* change.

Even if the laws remain the same, their interpretations by courts and administrative officials, often vary. In a federal system such as ours, there is a built-in problem since state and federal law differ, not to speak of the confusion between states. In addition, there are wide variations in the ways in which particular courts and administrative officials will interpret the same law at any given moment.

If you encounter what you consider to be a specific abuse of your rights, you should seek legal assistance. There are a number of agencies that may help you, among them, ACLU affiliate offices, but bear in mind that the ACLU is a limited-purpose organization. In many communities, there are federally funded legal service offices which provide assistance to persons who cannot afford the costs of legal representation. In general, the rights that the ACLU defends are freedom of inquiry and expression; due process of law; equal protection of the laws; and privacy. The authors in this series have discussed other rights (even though they sometimes fall outside the ACLU's usual concern) in order to provide as much guidance as possible.

These books have been planned as guides for the people directly affected; therefore, the question and answer format. (In some areas there are more detailed works available for "experts.") These guides seek to raise the major issues and inform the nonspecialist of the basic law on the subject. The authors of these books are themselves specialists who understand the need for information at "street level."

If you encounter a specific legal problem in an area discussed in one of these handbooks, show the book to your attorney. Of course, he or she will not be able to rely exclusively on the handbook to provide you with adequate representation. But if your attorney hasn't had a great deal of experience in the specific area, the handbook can provide helpful suggestions on how to proceed.

Norman Dorsen, President
American Civil Liberties Union

The principal purpose of this handbook, as well as others in this series, is to inform individuals of their legal rights. The authors from time to time suggest what the law should be, but their personal views are not necessarily those of the ACLU. For the ACLU's position on the issues discussed in this handbook, the reader should write to Librarian, ACLU, 132 West 43 Street, New York, NY 10036.

Introduction to the First Edition

Upon hearing that we were undertaking to write a book on the rights of gays, a wit remarked: "It must be a very short book." In fact, the book is relatively short. That is attributable, however, to how we have conceived our task and the uses to which we expect the book to be put, rather than to the absence of possible subject matter. It cannot be over-emphasized that we have not attempted to set forth in exhaustive or encyclopedic fashion, the unique problems that gay people are confronted with because of their sexual orientation; rather, we have endeavored to deal with only the most commonly occurring problems, and to sketch the impact of the law in those circumstances.

If there is a single, overriding lesson that emerges from the discussion that follows, it is that gay people do have a great many rights—indeed, the same rights as all other members of society—but that these rights take on significance only to the extent that they are intelligently and knowledgeably exercised. This means that at the moment your sexual orientation becomes an issue in the context of your employment, your familial relationships, housing, public accommodations, and so forth, you should secure the advice of counsel—either a lawyer, if a legal dispute is involved, or some other qualified person. A list of groups willing to assist in securing qualified counsel appears in the Appendix. Special note should be taken of the role of the American Civil Liberties Union in this respect. If you are being discriminated against because you are gay, or your sexual privacy is being invaded, we urge you to contact the local ACLU affiliate in your state. The addresses are found in the Appendix.

Your reading of this book will have been time well spent if it serves to impress on you the extent to which problems that you have are shared by others, and that the chance of successful resolution of those problems will be immeasurably enhanced if you do not attempt to go it alone.

One final caveat. The law is an ever-changing thing. It changes in response to shared perceptions of enlightened social policy and, significantly, in response to demands placed on it by those whom it affects. During the past decade, the laws applicable to the activities of gay people (both judge-made and statutory law) have been undergoing a revolution of sorts. Gay people are now conceded to have rights that were not conceived of ten or twenty years ago. This revolution has been spontaneous, however, only in the sense that its time had come; it did not simply happen, but was made to happen by vast numbers of people demanding, equitable treatment. We do not presume to have sufficient prescience to anticipate all future legal developments in this area. Instead, we have largely confined ourselves in this book to delineating the present state of the rights of gay people and to an occasional conjecture directed at how the laws can and, in our collective view, should develop.

We realize that there is a great deal of controversy over the nomenclature of the movement. Although we debated at length over the title of the book and the proper use of the words "gay," "lesbian," and "homosexual," we are aware that we still have not used words that will be universally acceptable. The word "homosexual" was used as infrequently as possible because many people contend that the name puts too much emphasis on the sexual aspect of gay relationships. But the courts still use the word, and consequently we must do so. We have used the word *gay*, to include gay men and lesbians, in the sincere hope that it will be useful to both.

Finally, we would like to dedicate the book to those people who have had the courage and the foresight to organize and speak out in defense of the rights of gay people.

The progress made over the past decade in the area of gay rights is attributable to their efforts, and it is to the continued efforts of like-minded people, that we must look for progress in the future.

E. CARRINGTON BOGGAN
MARILYN G. HAFT
CHARLES LISTER
JOHN P. RUPP

Introduction to the Second Edition

In the seven years since the publication of the first edition of this book, there have been many significant developments in the gay rights area, developments sufficient, in the view of the authors and editors, to warrant an updated edition.

More states have repealed laws prohibiting private consensual sexual conduct among adults, or have had such laws held unconstitutional as applied to private, consensual adult homosexual conduct; and more municipalities have adopted ordinances protecting gay people in employment, housing, and public accommodations—the first statewide law prohibiting such discrimination, has been adopted by Wisconsin. Court decisions have extended further protection to gay people in the military, and have affirmed their rights within the family. On the other hand, gay people continue to face a wide range of legal obstacles and discrimination in their daily lives that often require an alert understanding of their legal rights.

New developments have been incorporated into this revised edition in the hope that the book will better serve its readers, and to give encouragement to lesbians and gay men to persist in the continuing struggle for equal rights.

THOMAS B. STODDARD
E. CARRINGTON BOGGAN
MARILYN G. HAFT
CHARLES LISTER
JOHN P. RUPP

I

Freedom of Speech and Association: The Right to Organize and Speak Out

Until the late 1960s and early 1970s, gay men and women in the United States generally feared to speak out about their sexual orientation, or to organize groups to secure their legal rights. Indeed, the thought that gays even had rights that they could assert, did not occur to most people—gay or straight. The few organized groups that did exist, used names designed to conceal their homosexual nature so that prospective members would feel less uncomfortable about joining them. Only a very few individuals dared to speak out publicly in support of equal legal rights for gays.

In the late 1960s, the situation began to change dramatically. One of the events that provided a focal point for the gay movement as it exists today, was an event that has come to be known as the Stonewall Riots.[1] A gay bar on Christopher Street in New York's Greenwich Village, was raided by the police—a then-common occurrence—and the patrons fought back in an unprecedented assertion of the right of gay people to be free from unlawful police harassment. Shortly thereafter, the Gay Liberation Front was formed in New York City. It was one of the first organizations to use the word *gay* in its name. Similar groups have since appeared across the country, both in large and small cities and towns and on college campuses, openly referring to themselves as lesbian or gay organizations. Gay men and women have increasingly been willing to speak out in public, and to form groups in support of their right to be free from discrimination because of their

1

sexual orientation. The right of gays to organize and speak out
has not always been willingly conceded by society, however,
and resort to the courts has frequently been necessary to
redress discriminatory treatment.

Do gays have a right to form organizations for the purpose of securing equal treatment under the law?

Yes. Freedom of association is a right that flows from the
guarantees of freedom of assembly and speech, contained in
the First Amendment to the United States Constitution, and
the guarantee of liberty assured by the due process clause of
the Fourteenth Amendment. Courts have specifically acknowledged that the right of freedom of association extends to gay
organizations.[2]

Do gay organizations have the right to incorporate?

There is no reason why the legal benefits of incorporation
should not be available to gay organizations to the same
extent that they are available to any other organization, and
New York State's highest court has so held.[3] Gay organizations have been incorporated without any problems in many
other states.

May corporate status be denied a gay organization on the ground that its purposes offend "public policy"?

As long as the stated purposes of the organization do not
violate any law, corporate status should not be denied to a gay
organization on "public policy" grounds.[4] Such a rationale
would in fact be merely a subterfuge to conceal prejudice
against gays, and as such, should not be sanctioned by the
courts.[5] The New York court has so held.

For what purposes may gay organizations be formed?

Any lawful purpose, which includes advocating the change
or repeal of any existing law. When the Gay Activists Alliance
sought to incorporate in New York, the certificate of incorporation was initially rejected by the Secretary of State on the
grounds, among others, that "the purposes of the proposed
corporation raise serious questions as to whether it may be
formed to promote activitites which are contrary to public
policy and contrary to the penal laws of the State."[6] In
rejecting this rationale, a New York court held: "Generally,

they propose to allow assemblage of homosexuals to foster the repeal of certain laws which . . . discriminate against them as a class. It is well established that it is not unlawful for any individual or group of individuals to peaceably agitate for the repeal of any law."[7]

What are some of the specific purposes that have been upheld as proper and lawful for gay organizations?

The following purposes have all been upheld as lawful:[8]

1. To safeguard the rights guaranteed homosexual individuals by the constitutions and civil-rights laws of the United States and the several states through peaceful petition and assembly, and nonviolent protest, when necessary.

2. To speak out on public issues as a homosexual civil-rights organization working within the framework of the laws of the United States and the several states, but vigilant and vigorous in fighting any discrimination based on the sexual orientation of the individual.

3. To work for the repeal of all laws regulating sexual conduct and practices between consenting adults.

4. To work for the passage of laws ensuring equal treatment under the law of all persons regardless of sexual orientation.

5. To instill in homosexuals a sense of pride and self-worth.

6. To promote a better understanding of homosexuality among homosexuals and heterosexuals alike in order to achieve mutual respect, understanding, and friendship.

7. To hold meetings and social events for the better realization of the aforesaid purposes enunciated above and to achieve, ultimately, the complete liberation of homosexuals from all injustices visited upon them as such, that they may receive ultimate recognition as free and equal members of the human community.

Does the constitutionally protected right of association extend to gay student organizations at state-supported colleges and universities?

Yes. The right of freedom of association clearly extends to student organizations at state-supported institutions, subject to certain limitations deemed necessary for the preservation of the institution.[9] Several federal courts have explicitly applied this right to gay organizations at state-supported schools.[10]

Official school recognition of gay organizations cannot be withheld by officials at state-supported schools merely because they do not approve of the organization.

To what school benefits are such gay student organizations entitled?

The same benefits as any other officially recognized student organization. The benefits include the use of campus facilities for meetings and other appropriate purposes, and the right to use school media for the expression of ideas to the school community, and the community at large.[11]

Can gay student organizations sponsor and participate in social functions such as dances on the college or university campus?

Yes. A state-supported school must deal with student organizations in an evenhanded manner. Thus, if other student organizations, including those committed primarily to educational and political activities, are permitted the right to hold social functions, that right cannot be denied to gay student organizations.[12]

What criteria may legally be employed by a state-supported school to determine whether recognition may be denied to, or withdrawn from, a student organization?

There are three criteria that may lawfully be employed by school officials to evaluate any student organization: (1) failure or refusal to abide by reasonable "housekeeping" rules; (2) danger of violence or disruption of the university; and (3) violation of the criminal law by the organization or its members at functions sponsored by the organization.[13]

Is there anything inherent in a gay student organization that would come within any of these criteria?

No. The criteria basically require factual determinations in each particular case, and there is nothing in the nature of a gay organization per se, that would cause it to be in violation of any of these standards. In one case, a university contended that a gay organization's social functions were tantamount to criminal solicitation of deviate sexual relations, but the court found that there was no evidence that any unlawful activity was solicited or had occurred at any of the organization's functions.[14] (See the discussion of solicitation in chapter IX, "Gays and the Criminal Law.")

Does the freedom of association for gay students and gay student organizations extend to public high schools, as well as to colleges and universities?

Probably. "The relevant principles and rules [concerning students' rights] apply generally to both high schools and universities."[15] Thus, although there have as yet been no cases dealing specifically with the rights of gay public high school students to organize, it can be expected that the same principles will be applied to them, as to gay college or university students.

Does the constitutional guarantee of the right of association for gay organizations at state-supported schools, apply equally to gay organizations at private schools, colleges, and universities?

No. The constitutional protection against arbitrary interference with freedom of association applies only to schools run by the government—federal, state, or local. This is because the protections offered by the Constitution are against unlawful *state* action that interferes with fundamental rights, not against deprivation of those rights by private organizations. It is possible, however, that a private school might benefit from public programs of support (research or teaching grants, for example) to such a degree that its operations in fact become public. If this were to be found, the "private" school would become subject to the same restrictions as state-supported schools. For such a case to succeed, however, public support would have to be substantial.

Do gay organizations have a right to keep the names of their members confidential?

Under most circumstances, yes. The Supreme Court has held, that where, because of community temper, disclosure of the names of members of an organization might adversely affect those members, the organization is not required to disclose its membership list even if a state or local law requires it, or a governmental official demands it.[16] Forcing disclosure under such circumstances violates the members' freedom of association.[17] A gay person who feared that his membership in a gay organization might become known to others might not join the organization. However, competent legal advice should be obtained if a group confronts any official demand for its membership list.

Do gay organizations have to reveal the names of persons who make financial contributions to them or pay dues to them if required to do so pursuant to local or state laws?

Not usually. The Supreme Court has recognized that governmentally forced disclosure of contributors to organizations that espouse unpopular views can have a deterrent effect on the associational rights of the members of the organizations, and has ruled in general, that they may not be forced to divulge such information even if required to do so by local law.[18]

Would there ever be a circumstance under which a governmental body or official, could compel disclosure of the members of, or contributors to, a gay organization?

Yes. Although the Supreme Court has established a general rule whereby unpopular or unorthodox organizations can keep the names of their members and contributors secret, the Court has enunciated exceptions to this rule. If an organization seeks tax-exempt status, for example, it may have to divulge certain information on its sources of income. Moreover, an organization that actively participates in an election campaign, may be required to reveal the names of at least its major contributors under either the federal election laws, or state election laws.[19] Any gay organization faced with a demand for disclosure, should seek legal advice, for these are difficult legal issues and the law is not yet fully developed in this area. Any organization that intends to support a particular candidate, should, by all means, seek a lawyer's advice well before the campaign, so that it understands the implications of such activity.

Do members of a gay organization ever have a right to refuse to reveal their association with the organization to the government, and to prospective private employers?

Sometimes. The Supreme Court has held that while the Constitution unquestionably protects an individual from being forced to disclose his associational relationships in some circumstances, the right is not absolute, and where there is a state interest sufficiently compelling to overcome the individual's right to associational privacy, disclosure can be required.[20] A sufficiently compelling state interest would exist when the inquiry is related to the right of Congress to investigate Communist activity in the United States.[21] The Supreme Court upheld the dismissal of a public-school teacher for refusal to answer a question by his superintendent about his Communist activity.[22]

Indeed, public-school teachers face particularly difficult problems in this area. The Supreme Court has said that a public-school teacher does not give up the right to freedom of speech, belief, or association by teaching in the public schools, but he does have an obligation of "frankness, candor, and cooperation" in answering questions by the employing board because a teacher works in a sensitive area in the classroom, and shapes the attitude of young students toward society.[23]

In *Acanfora* v. *Board of Education of Montgomery County*,[24] a federal court of appeals upheld the transfer of a gay teacher from classroom to administrative duties on the grounds that he failed to reveal his participation in a gay student organization while in college, in a questionnaire concerning his extracurricular activities. The decision was based on grounds of misrepresentation.

Competent attorneys should be sought when trying to decide whether or not membership in a gay organization must be disclosed on an application form, or in an interview. Furthermore, it is important to remember that a right not to disclose, does not mean that there is a right to lie. False statements in response to official inquiries may give rise to civil liability, criminal penalties, or both.

May gay organizations obtain federal tax-exempt and tax-deductible status?

Yes. In 1978, the Internal Revenue Service issued a ruling whereby gay organizations could obtain tax-exempt, tax-deductible status if they otherwise qualify under the tax laws.[25] Since that time, the IRS has granted tax-exempt status to many different gay groups around the country.

It should be noted that there is nothing in the federal tax laws themselves that bars gay groups from tax-exempt status. The problem until recently was the IRS's interpretation of those laws.

What types of tax-deductible gay organizations presently exist?

At this time, there are tax-deductible gay organizations for religious purposes,[26] for legal advocacy and educational purposes,[27] and for scientific and educational purposes.[28]

May gay organizations receive government funds to conduct programs and projects?

Under most circumstances, they may. That is not to say, however, that it is easy for gay organizations to receive government grants. The government is reluctant to fund organizations that are in the least bit controversial.

Nonetheless, several gay organizations—most prominently, the Gay Community Services Center in Los Angeles—have succeeded in attracting government money.

In recent years, there have been several attempts to enact legislation, on both the federal and state levels, that would specifically bar government grants to gay organizations, and sometimes to gay individuals as well. For example, the so-called Family Protection Act, recently introduced in Congress, would (among other things) prohibit the dissemination of federal funds to any individual or group "for the purpose of advocating, promoting or suggesting homosexuality as a life-style."

A recent Florida Supreme Court case[29] indicates that the Family Protection Act, and similar proposals, are unconstitutional on First-Amendment grounds. That case involved a 1981 rider attached by the state legislature to a general appropriations bill that denied state funds to any college that gave official recognition or assistance to a group "that recommends or advocates sexual relations between persons not married to one another." The legislative history of the rider made it clear that the sponsors' true target was gay student organizations. The state supreme court struck down the rider only weeks after its passage on two grounds: first, that it was improper under a clause of the state constitution requiring that appropriations bills be limited to a single subject and, secondly, that it violated First-Amendment principles. As to the First Amendment, the court explained that it was well established that while the state could enact "reasonable regulations pertaining to [the] time, place and manner" of speech, it could not regulate speech on the basis of content, which the rider sought to do. The court added:

The right of persons to express themselves freely is not limited to statements of views that are acceptable to the majority of people. If it were to be held that freedom of expression applies only to views that the national, state, or local community finds to be within the range of reasonable discourse, the First Amendment would have little meaning or purpose.[30]

Do gay organizations have the right to provide legal services to their members to assist them in the assertion of their legal rights?

Yes. The Supreme Court has held that for minority groups seeking equal treatment under the law, association for litigation may be the most effective and sometimes the sole practicable form of political association and may not be abridged by governmental action.[31] "[C]ollective activity undertaken to obtain meaningful access to the courts is a fundamental right within the protection of the First Amendment."[32] The principle has been specifically found applicable to an organization formed for the purpose of protecting the legal rights of homosexuals.[33]

Do gays have a right to speak out publicly in support of their right to be gay, and in support of changing laws that discriminate against them?

Yes. The right to freedom of speech is one of the fundamental guarantees under the United States Constitution, and under all state constitutions. The right includes the advocacy of ideas and beliefs that may be unpopular with the majority. The only limitations are on words that amount to "incitement to imminent lawless action,"[34] "fighting words," that is, "words that by their very utterance inflict injury,[35] libel,[36] and obscenity.[37]"

Do gays have a right to assemble peacefully and to demonstrate in support of equal legal rights for homosexuals?

Yes. The First Amendment to the Constitution guarantees the rights to assemble peacefully, and to petition for the redress of grievances, and these rights include peaceful picketing and demonstrating.[38] Local officials who have attempted to abridge the right of gay organizations to demonstrate peacefully have been enjoined from doing so by the courts.[39]

Does the right of free speech include the right to distribute literature concerning gay issues?

Yes. The right to distribute circulars, handbills, or other literature advocating ideas and beliefs, is guaranteed as a corollary to freedom of speech and the press under the First Amendment to the Constitution.[40] While the right may be regulated by laws prohibiting littering, the basic right to distribute such material may not be abridged.

May the right to demonstrate peacefully and to picket in support of gay issues, be regulated at all?

Yes. While such activity may not be prohibited, it may be regulated in a nondiscriminatory way designed to promote public convenience.[41] The police may, for example, reasonably regulate the number of pickets in a given area.[42]

Does the right of free speech protect gay students and teachers in public schools and colleges from disciplinary action for wearing gay movement badges or buttons?

Yes. Wearing various items such as armbands and buttons that have a symbolic meaning, is a form of free speech called symbolic speech. Symbolic speech is an act that, although not necessarily exclusively speech, is nonetheless a public expression of belief or opinion, and it comes within the protection of the free-speech clause of the First Amendment.[43] Such symbolic acts are generally protected by the Constitution, from governmental interference, including interference by school officials. In upholding the right of high-school students to wear armbands protesting the Vietnam War, for example, the Supreme Court stated that "[i]t can hardly be argued that either students or teachers shed their constitutional rights to freedom of expression at the schoolhouse gate."[44] The right of students to wear "freedom buttons" has also been specifically upheld where the students wearing the buttons were not engaged in any disruptive activities.[45] The principles of these cases would appear to apply equally to those wearing the symbols of the gay movement. Mere fear on the part of school officials that to permit students to wear such items, would cause a disturbance, is not sufficient justification for prohibiting such free expression or for disciplining it. "[I]n our system, undifferentiated fear or apprehension of disturbance is not enough to overcome the right to freedom of expression. . . . [O]ur Constitution says we must take this risk."[46]

In practice, it should be noted, *teachers* may have a more difficult time enforcing their rights to wear symbols of the gay movement in school.

May a gay public-school teacher be dismissed or transferred to nonteaching duties for exercising freedom of speech on gay issues outside the classroom?

Usually not. It has been held that the transfer of a gay teacher to nonteaching duties could not be sustained on the grounds that he appeared on television and made other public statements in support of his right to teach.[47] The Supreme Court had previously held that while a teacher's right to freedom of speech may be balanced against the importance the state properly attaches to the uninterrupted education of its youth, a teacher's comments on public issues that are neither knowingly false, nor made in reckless disregard of the truth, afford no ground for dismissal when they do not impair the teacher's performance of his or her duties, or interfere with the operation of the schools.[48]

In 1977, a federal court ordered a gay college teacher reinstated after he was dismissed for making statements about homosexuality.[49]

Have the courts uniformly upheld those who speak out on gay rights to be free from governmental reprisals?

Not always. The law concerning gay rights is still very much in a developing stage. A federal court of appeals has thus upheld the refusal of a state university to employ a gay person, otherwise completely qualified, as head of the university library's cataloging division.[50] The grounds for the refusal were that the applicant's "personal conduct, as represented in the public and University news media, is not consistent with the best interest of the University."[51] James McConnell, the applicant, a gay man, had applied for a marriage license to marry another gay man, and the event received much publicity. The university's refusal to employ McConnell was challenged on the grounds that it was based on his desire to profess publicly his earnest belief that homosexuals are entitled to privileges equal to those afforded heterosexuals. A lower federal court agreed with this position and enjoined the university from refusing to hire McConnell.[52]

The court of appeals agreed with the university, however, and reversed the lower court ruling.[53] The court of appeals' decision clearly indicates that the refusal to hire was not sustained merely on the basis of McConnell's homosexuality, but flowed directly from his outspoken public posture and activism on behalf of gay rights. McConnell was thus penalized for exercising freedom of speech and association on behalf of gay rights. The result is in conflict with other federal court decisions that maintain that a gay person cannot be penalized for exercising First-Amendment rights to freedom of speech and association.[54] It may be hoped that other courts will ultimately adopt the latter position.

Are there any reported cases of the First-Amendment rights of gay high-school students?

Yes. In a fascinating federal district court case in 1980, a gay high-school student in Rhode Island brought suit to force his principal to allow him to take another male to the school prom as his date. The court accepted his argument that the proposed conduct constituted "symbolic speech" under the First Amendment, and ordered the principal to permit him to attend.[55]

May public facilities that accept advertising dealing with social or political issues, refuse to accept advertising from gay rights organizations?

No. A federal court has held that where a public transportation authority accepted other advertisements espousing controversial political and social concerns, it created a public forum, and access to such a public forum could be limited only by precise, clear regulations concerning time, place, and manner of speech. Access to such a forum could not be barred because gay rights views might be unpopular.[56]

Must radio and television broadcasters include the gay community in ascertaining community needs in public affairs and news programs?

Yes. The Federal Communications Commission has ordered that all licensed broadcasters must include the gay community in ascertaining community needs in public affairs and news programs, provided that the particular local gay community served by a broadcaster, can demonstrate that it is a significant element of the community.[57] This ruling will provide gays with greater access to the media for the presentation of programming about gay concerns.

NOTES

1. See generally Teal, *The Gay Militants* (1971); Altman, *Homosexual Oppression and Liberation*, Ch. 4 (1971); Lauristen and Thorstad, *The Homosexual Rights Movement* [1864–1935] (1973).
2. Gay Students Organization v. Bonner, 367 F. Supp. 1088 (D.N.H.), *aff'd*, 509 F.2d 652 (1st Cir. 1974); Gay Activists Alliance v. Lomenzo, 38 A.D. 2d 981, 329 N.Y.S. 2d 181 (3d Dept. 1972), *aff'd*, 31 N.Y. 2d 965, 341 N.Y.S. 2d 108 (1973).
3. Gay Activists Alliance v. Lomenzo, *supra* note 2.
4. *Id.*
5. *Id.*
6. 329 N.Y.S. 2d at 182.
7. *Id.* at 183.
8. *Id.* at 183.
9. Healy v. James, 408 U.S. 169 (1971); Gay Students Organization v. Bonner, *supra* note 2.
10. Gay Students Organization v. Bonner, *supra* note 2; Gay Alliance of Students v. Matthews, 544 F.2d 162 (4th Cir. 1976); Gay Lib v. University of Missouri, 558 F.2d 848 (8th Cir. 1977), *cert denied*, *sub nom.* Ratchford v. Gay Lib, 434 U.S. 1080 (1978) (with forceful dissent by Rehnquist, J.); Student Coalition for Gay Rights v. Austin Peay State University, 477 F. Supp. 1267 (M.D. Tenn. 1979).
11. Healy v. James, *supra* note 9.
12. Gay Students Organization v. Bonner, *supra* note 2.
13. Healy v. James, *supra* note 9.
14. Gay Students Organization v. Bonner, *supra* note 2.
15. Scoville v. Board of Education, 425 F.2d 10, 13 n. 5 (7th Cir. 1970).
16. NAACP v. Alabama, 357 U.S. 449 (1958).
17. Bates v. Little Rock, 361 U.S. 516 (1960).
18. Buckley v. Valeo, 424 U.S. 1 (1976).
19. *Id.*
20. Barenblatt v. United States, 360 U.S. 109 (1959).
21. *Id.*; Wilkinson v. United States, 365 U.S. 399 (1961); Braden v. United States, 365 U.S. 431 (1961).
22. Beilan v. Board of Education, 357 U.S. 399 (1958).
23. *Id.* at 405.

24. Acanfora v. Board of Education of Montgomery County, 491 F.2d 498 (4th Cir. 1974).
25. IRB 1978–33, Rev. Rul. 78–305.
26. Metropolitan Community Church.
27. Lambda Legal Defense & Education Fund, Inc.
28. Erickson Foundation; Institute for Human Identity.
29. Department of Education v. Lewis, 416 So. 2d 4 55 (1982).
30. *Id.* at 461.
31. United Transportation Union v. State Bar of Michigan, 401 U.S. 576 (1971). See also Brotherhood of Railroad Trainmen v. Virginia State Bar, 377 U.S. 1 (1964); United Mine Workers v. Illinois State Bar Association, 389 U.S. 217 (1967).
32. United Transportation Union v. State Bar of Michigan, *supra* note 31, at 585.
33. Application of Thom, 33 N.Y. 2d 609, 347 N.Y.S. 2d 571, 575 (1973) (Burke, J., concurring).
34. Brandenburg v. Ohio, 395 U.S. 444 (1969).
35. Chaplinsky v. New Hampshire, 315 U.S. 568 (1942).
36. New York Times Co. v. Sullivan, 376 U.S. 255 (1964).
37. Miller v. California, 413 U.S. 15 (1973).
38. Thornhill v. Alabama, 310 U.S. 88 (1940); Schneider v. Irvington, 308 U.S. 147 (1939).
39. Gay Activists Alliance v. Murphy, Unreported mem. decision (S.D.N.Y. 1972).
40. Schneider v. Irvington, 308 U.S. 147 (1939).
41. Cox v. Louisiana, 379 U.S. 536 (1964).
42. *Id.*
43. West Virginia v. Barnette, 319 U.S. 624 (1943).
44. Tinker v. Des Moines Independent Community School District, 393 U.S. 503, 506 (1969).
45. Burnside v. Byars, 363 F.2d 744 (5th Cir. 1966).
46. Tinker v. Des Moines Independent Community School District, *supra* note 44, at 508.
47. Acanfora v. Board of Education, *supra* note 24.
48. Pickering v. Board of Education, 391 U.S. 563 (1968).
49. Aumiller v. University of Delaware, 434 F. Supp. 1273 (D. Del. 1977). But see National Gay Task Force v. Board of Education, No. Civ-80-1174-E (W.D. Okla. June 29, 1982), in whch a federal district court judge upheld the constitutionality of a recently-enacted Oklahoma statute authorizing the dismissal of any teacher "advocating, soliciting, imposing, encouraging or promoting public or private homosexual activity in a manner that creates a substantial risk that such conduct will come to the attention of school children or school employees." However, in so doing, he determined that the statute would not allow a school board to dismiss a teacher for merely

discussing homosexuality openly, or for advocating equality for, or tolerance of homosexuals.

50. McConnell v. Anderson, 451 F.2d 193 (8th Cir. 1971), *cert. denied*, 405 U.S. 1046 (1972).

51. *Id.* at 194.

52. McConnell v. Anderson, 316 F. Supp. 809 (D. Minn.), *rev'd* 451 F.2d 193 (8th Cir. 1971).

53. McConnell v. Anderson, *supra* note 50, at 196.

54. See, e.g. Acanfora v. Board of Education, *supra* note 24; Van Ooteghem v. Gray, 628 F. 2d 488 (5th Cir.), *aff'd en banc*, 654 F.2d 304 (5th Cir. 1981), *cert. denied*, 102 S. Ct. 1255 (1982). But see Singer v. U.S. Civil Service Commission, 530 F.2d 247 (9th Cir. 1976), *vacated as moot*, 429 U.S. 1034 (1977).

55. Fricke v. Lynch, 491 F. Supp. 381 (D.R.I. 1980), *vacated and remanded*, 627 F.2d 1088 (1st Cir. 1981).

56. Gay Activists Alliance v. Washington Metropolitan Area Transit Authority, 48 U.S.L.W. 2053 (D.D.C. 1979). See also Alaska Gay Coalition v. Sullivan, 578 P.2d 951 (Ala. 1978).

57. *The Advocate,* Apr. 17, 1980, 7.

II

The Right to Equal
Employment Opportunities

The law long ago abandoned the notion that employment is a matter that should be left exclusively to agreements between workers and employers. Legislators and judges now generally recognize that many aspects of the employment relationship must be regulated for the protection of the worker. In particular, it is now widely acknowledged that society should undertake to assure all citizens fair-employment opportunities that are consistent with their training and abilities. A series of federal and state statutes now provide varying degrees of protection against employment discrimination on the basis of race, sex, or age. However, the law still offers little protection against discrimination on the basis of sexual preferences. As a general matter, such protection is provided only in two situations: where government itself is the employer, and where a local government has forbidden discrimination by private employers on the basis of sexual preferences. The protection is partial and inadequate, but more effective controls are likely to be obtained only by legislation.

May private employers lawfully discriminate against employees on the basis of sexual preference?
In most situations, yes. At present, federal legislation protects women, racial minorities, and certain other groups, but not gays. A bill that would outlaw discrimination on the basis of "affectional or sexual orientation," has been pending in Congress for several years, but the chance of passage still

seems remote. And the courts have so far rejected the theory that the federal prohibition on sex discrimination (Title VII of the Civil Rights Act of 1964) also covers sexual orientation.[1]

One state, Wisconsin, now has a statewide statute banning discrimination on the basis of sexual preference, and so do many municipalities, including Los Angeles, Philadelphia, San Francisco, Minneapolis, and Washington, D.C. (Lamentably, some other cities—Miami and St. Paul are the best known—once had protective ordinances that were subsequently modified or repealed in local elections.)

Without such local legislation, only two possible avenues of relief against a private employer are available. First, it is possible, although unlikely, that such discrimination may be forbidden by an applicable employment contract. The possibility should be explored with a qualified legal adviser or, if you are a union member, with your union representative. Second, it may be possible to initiate litigation to establish that the employer's conduct violated a right guaranteed by the Constitution. The probability of success in such litigation is not encouraging. It would first be necessary to establish that the employer's business was sufficiently related to governmental activities, to bring it within the constitutional restrictions which apply solely to government action. It would also be necessary to show that the employer's discriminatory conduct was arbitrary and capricious.

One such case, involving a public telephone company, recently resulted in a major victory for gay people in California. In that case, the California Supreme Court held that the company's activities were so closely intertwined with the state government, and so important to the public welfare, that it was quasi-governmental in character. The court then ruled that the company's arbitrary exclusion of qualified gay people from employment opportunities violated the equal protection guarantee of the California state constitution, as well as certain state statutes.[2]

The decision is heartening, and the court's opinion contains some stirring language, but it should be noted, that the decision is based on previous California caselaw on "state-protected quasi-monopolies" like the telephone company, caselaw which does not generally exist in other states.

May governmental employers discriminate against employees on the basis of sexual orientation?

As a general rule, no. Governmental employers—whether local, state, or federal—are subject to constitutional requirements that they act fairly and evenhandedly toward all citizens. Those requirements do not demand that governmental agencies act identically with respect to all citizens. It is generally sufficient if any differences in treatment have some rational relationship to the purposes of the governmental program involved. With respect to matters of employment, this generally means that any differences in treatment must bear some rational relationship to the efficiency or effectiveness with which government work may be performed.

The principles applicable here have been developed chiefly in connection with federal employment. Section 3301 of Title 5 of the United States Code provides the basic standard for regulating federal employment. The section states that the president may prescribe such regulations for the admission of individuals into the Civil Service as "will best promote the efficiency of that service." The section also provides that the president may ascertain the fitness of applicants "as to age, health, character, knowledge, and ability for the employment sought." Pursuant to this statutory authorization, the Civil Service Commission has issued regulations that require federal employees and applicants for employment to provide certain information, and that create various mandatory standards of conduct for employees.

The regulations used to forbid "criminal, infamous, dishonest, immoral, or notoriously disgraceful conduct." Under those regulations, the Civil Service Commission has in the past sought to exclude from federal employment those who have engaged in homosexual conduct. As described below, the regulations have since been revised by the Commission.

What is the Civil Service Commission's present attitude?

In December of 1973, in response to a number of successful law suits brought by federal employees who had been wrongly dismissed, the commission issued the following directive to federal supervisors:

[Y]ou may not find a person unsuitable for Federal employment merely because that person is a homosexual or has engaged in homosexual acts, nor may such exclusion be based on a conclusion that a homosexual person might bring the public service into public contempt. You are, however, permitted to dismiss a person or find him or her unsuitable for Federal employment where the evidence establishes that such person's homosexual conduct affects job fitness—excluding from such consideration, however, unsubstantiated conclusions concerning possible embarrassment to the Federal Service.[3]

This directive, which is still in effect, recognizes that the suitability of employees must be determined individually, and not on the supposed characteristics of an entire class of persons. It is no guarantee of job security for gay workers, but it constitutes a substantial improvement in the law.

Congress enacted a Civil Service Reform Act in 1978. The act makes no specific mention of homosexuality, but it does state that supervisors may not discriminate "on the basis of conduct which does not adversely affect the performance of the employee or applicant or the performance of others."[4] This statutory change would seem to enhance further the employment rights of federal workers who happen to be gay.

What should federal employees do if they are confronted with the accusation that they engaged in homosexual conduct?

It is always best, whenever possible, to refuse to answer questions or to provide information until you have consulted with an attorney or other qualified adviser. A federal employee is, however, required by civil service regulations, to provide information reasonably related to the employee's fitness for federal employment, and it is important to avoid an absolute refusal to provide such information. The commission's rights of inquiry are matters of continuing dispute, and decisions whether to give or to refuse to give it information, should be made carefully and only after qualified advice has been obtained.[5] Do not provide false or misleading information, but do not let yourself be forced into admissions of guilt.

Have the courts imposed restrictions on efforts to discriminate against federal employees on the basis of sexual preference?

The courts have traditionally deferred to an administrative

agency's decision on the reasonableness of the grounds for dismissal,[6] and have accordingly been reluctant to interfere with dismissals for homosexual conduct. Indeed, until recently, the agency would only have to adhere to the procedures required by statute and regulation. In 1950, however, the Court of Claims held that employees should be permitted to show that, apart from any procedural deficiencies, a dismissal was arbitrary and capricious.[7]

Over the past fifteen years, on the basis of that important ruling, courts have gradually imposed a series of important restrictions on efforts to discriminate against federal employees on the basis of sexual preference. In 1969, the United States Court of Appeals for the District of Columbia, perhaps the second most important federal court in the country, held that although the Civil Service Commission has wide discretion with respect to employment decisions, the agency may dismiss an employee suspected of homosexual conduct only when it can prove that its action will promote the efficiency of the civil service.[8] More importantly, the court indicated that it would inquire closely into the adequacy of the nexus between the alleged misconduct, and the efficiency of the agency. It also totally rejected the idea that merely because conduct may be styled "immoral," there is an adequate cause for removal. It said:

> We are not prepared to say that the Commission could not reasonably find appellant's homosexual advance to be "immoral," "indecent," or "notoriously disgraceful" under dominant conventional norms. But the notion that it could be an appropriate function of the federal bureaucracy to enforce the majority's conventional codes of conduct in the private lives of its employees is at war with elementary concepts of liberty, privacy, and diversity.

The decisions in this and subsequent cases,[9] represent major steps forward. The courts have rejected the most blatant forms of discrimination, and have provided a framework in order to achieve further progress. Nonetheless, many judges and administrators do not share the views expressed in these cases, and it is clear that more litigation will be necessary. It is likely that future litigation will turn on the specific facts of each employee's situation, rather than broad issues of the commission's authority. It should be anticipated that the government will, from time to time, seek other evidence of alleged instability or misconduct to justify dismissals, and gay employees may find that any emotional or other difficulties, however common or trivial, may be used to support dismissals.

Do these same principles also apply to employment with state and local governments?

Many of the cases involving federal employment have relied on the specific provisions of federal statutes and regulations. State and local governments have separate statutes and regulations, and certain issues may as a result, be different. Nonetheless, the underlying constitutional principles remain largely the same, and state and local government employees should also be protected against arbitrary dismissals and exclusions. As a practical matter, however, litigation regarding state and local employees has not yet been extensive, and the applicable principles have been less fully developed in that context.

Are teaching and other positions in the public schools also governed by these same principles?

As a general matter, the same principles should be applicable, but many courts are particularly hostile to the employment of gays as teachers,[10] due to a fear of "contagion." Any evidence, or suggestion, that students may be influenced by a teacher's sexual preferences, is considered sufficient, by some judges, to sustain a dismissal. On the other hand, the boards of education of the District of Columbia and New York City, among other places, have abandoned or modified their efforts to exclude gay teachers and other school employees. As this suggests, in some cities progress may be made more easily through quiet and informal understandings with local authorities, than through the courts or through legislation.

The basic rules applicable here were concisely stated by the Supreme Court of California in 1969, in a case in which the court overturned the dismissal of a public-school teacher because of homosexual conduct.[11] The court held that "immoral conduct" permits the dismissal of a teacher only when an unfitness to teach can be proven. In determining fitness, the court held that the state board of education may take into account such matters as adverse consequences on students or other teachers, the degree of such adversity, the recency of the conduct, the motive, the likelihood of recurrence, and the extent to which disciplinary action may have an adverse impact on the exercise of constitutional rights. In the court's view, the law neither prohibits the employment of gay persons, nor forbids educational authorities to consider the possible implications of homosexuality, in order to determine a teacher's fitness.

The strength of feeling against the employment of gay persons in educational positions, is suggested by a 1971 case in a federal court of appeals. The court upheld the refusal of the University of Minnesota to employ a widely known gay activist in the university library.[12] It reversed the decision of a federal district court[13] that held that the university had acted arbitrarily. The court of appeals emphasized that the university's board of regents has broad discretion with respect to such matters, and that its discretion should not be disturbed in the absence of a "clear and affirmative" showing of arbitrariness. The court thought it quite reasonable to reject the applicant because he sought actively to "implement" his sexual preferences, and his employment by the university would place its "tacit approval" on the "socially repugnant concept" that the applicant represented. The court appeared to be disturbed not only by the applicant's sexual preferences, but also by his unwillingness to hide them.

What if the teacher lies about his or her sexual preferences?
The teacher's dismissal may be based on such a lie or deliberate omission. For example, a federal court of appeals in 1974, upheld the dismissal of a public-school teacher for such an omission.[14] The court rejected the claim, which had been adopted by the district court, that the teacher should be denied reinstatement because of public statements he had made after his removal. Nonetheless, the court emphasized that the teacher had deliberately failed to provide information regarding his sexual preferences and associations at the time of his original employment, and held that this prevented him from challenging the school system's refusal to employ gays as teachers.

NOTES

1. See DeSantis v. Pacific Telephone and Telegraph Co., 608 F.2d 327 (9th Cir. 1979); Smith v. Liberty Mutual Insurance Co., 395 F. Supp. 1098 (N.D. Ga. 1975). Cf. Macauley v. Massachusetts Com-

mission Against Discrimination, 397 N.E. 2d 670 (Mass. 1979) (the Massachusetts statute prohibiting discrimination on the basis of sex does not include sexual preference).

2. Gay Law Students Association v. Pacific Telephone and Telegraph Co., 24 Cal. 3d 458, 595 P.2d 592, 156 Cal. Rptr. 14 (1979).

3. Civil Service Bulletin, Dec. 21, 1973, quoted in Ashton v. Civiletti, 613 F.2d 923, 927 (D.C. Cir. 1979).

4. 5 U.S.C. §2302(b) (10).

5. See generally Richardson v. Hampton, 345 F. Supp. 600 (D.D.C. 1972). In 1980, the federal Office of Personnel Management issued a new policy directing supervisors not to make inquiries into non-job-related conduct, including sexual orientation. Memorandum, Policy Statement on Discrimination on the Basis of Conduct Which Does Not Adversely Affect the Performance of Employees or Applicants for Employment (OPM, May 12, 1980), at 2.

6. See generally Bailey v. Richardson, 182 F.2d 46 (D.C. Cir. 1950), *aff'd per curiam*, 341 U.S. 918 (1951).

7. Gadsden v. United States, 78 F. Supp. 126 (Ct. Cl. 1948), *cert. denied*, 342 U.S. 856 (1951).

8. Norton v. Macy, 417 F.2d 1161 (D.C. Cir. 1969). See generally Note, *Government-Created Employment Disabilities of the Homosexual*, 82 Harv. L. Rev. 1738 (1969); Comment, *Homosexuals in Government Employment*, 3 Seton Hall L. Rev. 87 (1971); Siniscalco, *Homosexual Discrimination in Employment*, 16 Santa Clara L. Rev. 495 (1976).

9. See, e.g. Society for Individual Rights, Inc. v. Hampton, 63 F.R.D. 399 (N.D. Cal. 1973), *aff'd on other grounds*, 528 F.2d 905 (9th Cir. 1975); Ashton v. Civiletti, 613 F.2d 923 (D.C. Cir. 1979).

10. See, e.g. Gaylord v. Tacoma School District No. 10, 88 Wash. 2d 286, 559 P.2d 1340 (1977), *cert. denied*, 98 S. Ct. 234 (1977).

11. Morrison v. State Board of Education, 1 Cal. 3d 214, 461 P.2d 375, 82 Cal. Rptr. 175 (1969).

12. McConnell v. Anderson, 451 F.2d 193 (8th Cir. 1971), *cert denied*, 405 U.S. 1046 (1972). See also National Gay Task Force v. Board of Education, discussed in chapter I, note 49.

13. McConnell v. Anderson, 316 F. Supp. 809 (D. Minn. 1970).

14. Acanfora v. Board of Education, 491 F.2d 498 (4th Cir.), *cert. denied*, 419 U.S. 836 (1974).

III

Occupational Licenses

An additional species of employment restriction stems from the authority of state governments and, derivatively, of lesser governmental entities such as counties and municipalities, to require people in certain occupations to be licensed. Occupational licensing laws, and agencies to enforce those laws, exist in every state. The result is a network of restrictions covering a broad range of extremely diverse occupations.

Occupational licensing laws often are administered in such a way, that the employment opportunities of gay people are restricted. Such laws are almost invariably justified in terms of the public's interest in ensuring that people in certain occupations are adequately trained, and at least minimally honest and reliable. In practice, however, the laws tend to be used as vehicles for enforcing majority social and political views.

What is an occupational license?

An occupational license generally takes the form of a certificate awarded by a state, county, or municipality, attesting that the requirements for engaging in a designated occupation, are satisfied. Many occupational licensing laws absolutely prohibit people from performing certain activities unless they have been specifically authorized to do so—for example, those that control entry into the fields of medicine and law. Other licensing laws simply prohibit people from describing their services to the public without official authorization—for example, some laws reserve the title "licensed practical nurse," to people who have obtained an appropriate license.

Although licensees are permitted to practice only in the licensing state, reciprocity agreements are now in effect for many occupations; people who have been licensed in one jurisdiction, are able to move to another jurisdiction without having to reapply. Although many licenses are effective so long as the conditions set out by the licensing authority are complied with, others require periodic updating or reapplication. Rarely may licenses be transferred from one person to another without the approval of the licensing authority.

Occupational licensing should not be confused with the certification programs. Occupational licensing is a species of government regulation; failure to comply is illegal. Certification programs, by contrast, are voluntary; they are simply a means by which a nongovernmental body may grant special recognition to people possessing certain qualifications. For example, the American Medical Association may certify that a person is a qualified surgeon, and a bar unit may certify that a lawyer is a trial specialist.

How many occupations are subject to licensing restrictions?

At last count, approximately three hundred fifty occupations were covered by licensing restrictions in one or more states.[1] Some of these, such as medicine and law, are always subject to licensing restrictions. Many other occupations are subject to licensing restrictions in only one or a few states. It has been estimated that some seven million people in the United States are presently working in licensed occupations; the vast majority are in occupations to which entry is absolutely prohibited without a license.

What is the source of the authority exercised by states and other governmental entities requiring occupational licenses?

The Supreme Court held in *Dent* v. *West Virginia*, that "the power of the State to provide for the general welfare of its people authorizes it to prescribe all such regulations as, in its judgment, will secure or tend to secure them against the consequences of ignorance and incapacity as well as of deception and fraud."[2] This authority is exceedingly broad. In fact, until comparatively recently, courts rarely have struck down licensing restrictions or overturned licensing decisions since these fall within the power of the states.

Counties and municipalities can impose licensing restrictions within their jurisdictions only if that authority has been delegated to them, either expressly or by implication, by the state.

How are occupational licensing restrictions enforced?

Virtually every jurisdiction that has enacted occupational licensing restrictions also has created boards or agencies to administer them. These entities may be either quite passive (amounting to little more than an informational clearinghouse), or very active and intrusive.

Most of these boards or agencies are composed exclusively or predominantly, of members of the licensed occupation. The justification for this is that the demands and problems of individual occupations can be understood best by people working in the occupation itself. But self-regulation necessarily entails a conflict of interest, since potential competition will be eliminated. Of perhaps greater pertinence, so far as gays are concerned, is that self-regulation has often operated to reinforce occupational conservatism—reflected in the notion that a legitimate function of a licensing agency is to exclude persons who, because of some characteristic not consistent with majoritarian values, may bring the occupation into public disrepute.

Many statutes and ordinances provide that anyone who works without a license in an occupation where it is required, commits a crime, and persons engaging in such prohibited conduct may be fined or imprisoned.

What forms do occupational licensing restrictions normally take?

As already noted, some restrictions absolutely prohibit unlicensed persons from engaging in particular occupations, while others simply prohibit people from describing their services to the public in a certain way. Beyond that, licensing restrictions may be characterized as either minimum "standards," or "prohibitions." Occupational standards normally have an age, education, skill, or experience requirement. The technical competence of applicants often is measured by a written examination; a prerequisite to this examination might be the completion of a required course of study.

Prohibitions restricting initial or continued access to certain occupations generally take one of four often overlapping forms:

1. Provisions referring to the conviction or commission of a criminal offense (a misdemeanor or, more often, a felony).
2. Provisions referring to the conviction of a criminal or civil offense involving "moral turpitude."
3. Provisions giving licensing boards or agencies wide discretion to deny occupational licenses to, and to suspend the licenses of, those found not to possess "good moral character."
4. Provisions relating to other types of unprofessional or negligent conduct.

What special problems are gays confronted with regarding occupational licenses?

Most of the unique problems confronted by gay people in securing and retaining occupational licenses relate to what we have characterized as licensing "prohibitions." Gays have been excluded from a variety of occupations on the grounds that their sexual orientation or activities are indicative of a degenerate moral character. Occupational licenses can be denied or revoked if one is convicted of homosexual activity on the grounds that such offenses involve moral turpitude.

The vagueness of the phrases *good moral character* and *moral turpitude*, virtually ensures the unfair application of licensing restrictions to gays. The experiences of gay people in applying for occupational licenses, or in attempting to retain such licenses after the fact of their sexual orientation has been communicated to the relevant licensing authority, have varied widely.

It is difficult to tote up the experiences of gay people before licensing boards or agencies, or to discern patterns, because individual decisions are seldom published. In addition, the criteria employed by licensing authorities in reaching decisions, if written at all, are not widely circulated. Nevertheless, a few generalizations are possible:

1. Although actual figures may not be available, the vast majority of gays who seek occupational licenses do not experience unique problems. Similarly, most gays who obtain

occupational licenses retain them without difficulty. The reason is that most licensing authorities do not actively solicit information concerning sexual orientation. But, gay people have experienced problems when the licensing authority learns of their sexual orientation.

2. The access of gays to sensitive or "public interest" occupations such as teaching or law, traditionally has been more restricted than access to other occupations. Particularly when the occupation has involved contact with young people, licensing boards and agencies have tended to deny licenses whenever sexual orientation somehow has become an issue, generally on the grounds that the public has a significant interest in minimizing such contact because of the vulnerability of young people to "immoral influences."

3. The likelihood that an applicant's sexual orientation will become an issue during the licensing process, increases measurably if the applicant has been arrested for, or convicted of, a criminal offense due to homosexual activity. Many licensing bodies equate those incidents as conclusive evidence of moral turpitude.

4. Some licensing bodies have been willing to disregard homosexual conduct if the applicant has been able to demonstrate that the conduct was aberrational. The age of the applicant when the homosexual conduct took place, is also taken into consideration. Whether the applicant had been drinking, and whether the activity was private or consensual (without force or fraud by the applicant), have also been regarded as relevant to a determination of the fitness of the applicant.

If in the process of applying for an occupational license, or while holding a license, my sexual orientation becomes an issue, what should I do?

The first thing to do is to retain a qualified attorney. Most licensing bodies are required by statute or ordinance to afford applicants and license holders certain procedural rights while considering whether to award, suspend, or revoke a license. At least in cases in which all licensing "standards" have been met, the Due Process Clause of the Constitution probably would require the licensing authority to hold a hearing before denying or revoking an occupational license because your conduct ran afoul of one of the "prohibitions" listed above.[3]

One important service a lawyer can render is to ensure that you have taken advantage of all procedural rights. Counsel also can make sure that your situation is communicated to the licensing body in a favorable manner. If there are exceptional circumstances that might be relevant, those circumstances should be presented. A lawyer can also help to ensure that your right to personal privacy is not unduly invaded in the process. Finally, a lawyer can advise you on any right of judicial review if the licensing authority decides against you. It is important to keep the possibility of judicial review in mind during the proceedings before the licensing body, since the record made before that body, will form the core of such review.

How have challenges to the denial or revocation of occupational licenses fared in the courts?

Courts traditionally have been reluctant to substitute their judgment concerning a person's fitness to engage in a particular occupation, for the judgment of licensing boards and agencies.[4] That reluctance appears to be eroding somewhat; an increasing number of recent cases have been reported, in which courts have held licensing decisions to have been arbitrary and unreasonable, and in contravention of legal rights.

A major case in recent years is *Schware* v. *Board of Bar Examiners*.[5] *Schware* challenged the refusal of the New Mexico Board of Bar Examiners to permit an applicant to take the bar examination on the grounds that the applicant had not demonstrated "good moral character." The Board of Bar Examiners relied on the fact that the applicant had used several aliases some twenty years prior to his application, had been arrested (but not convicted) some seventeen years before, and had been a member of the Communist party. In reversing the board's decision, the Supreme Court stated:

A state cannot exclude a person from the practice of law or from any other occupation in a manner or for reasons that contravene the Due Process or Equal Protection Clauses of the Fourteenth Amendment.

A state can require high standards or qualifications, such as good moral character or proficiency in its laws before it admits an applicant to the bar, but any qualification must have a rational connection with the applicant's fitness or capacity to practice. . . . [6]

More recently, in *Morrison* v. *State Board of Education*,[7] a case involving the revocation of a teaching license because of an isolated incident of homosexual conduct, the California Supreme Court held that the terms "unprofessional," "moral turpitude," and "immoral," were too vague. In reaching that conclusion, the court noted:

> Terms such as "immoral or unprofessional conduct" or "moral turpitude" stretch over so wide a range that they embrace an unlimited area of conduct. In using them the Legislature surely did not mean to endow the employing agency with the power to dismiss any employee whose personal, private conduct incurred its disapproval. Hence the courts have consistently related the terms to the issue of whether, when applied to the performance of the employee on the job, the employee has disqualified himself.[8]

The court in *Morrison* went on to state that "[t]he right to practice one's profession is sufficiently precious to surround it with a panoply of legal protection. . . ."[9] Since the board had not conducted an inquiry into the petitioner's fitness to teach required by the Constitution and state statute, the court reversed the board's decision revoking the petitioner's teaching certificate.

The decision of the California Supreme Court in the *Morrison* case, as well as decisions in other recent cases such as *Board of Education* v. *Jack M.*,[10] *Application of Kimball*,[11] and *In re Florida Board of Bar Examiners*,[12] may well stimulate other courts to look more carefully at decisions by licensing authorities in cases involving homosexuality. The fact that several state legislatures and municipal governing bodies have eased licensing restrictions previously applicable to gays, is an encouraging sign that more widespread legislative changes benefiting gays will be enacted.

At the same time, however, it is important to recognize that progress in this area has been slow; at all levels—administrative, legislative, and judicial—licensing decisions

adverse to gays, have continued to occur.[13] The best advice
thus remains: if you apply for, or are holding an occupational
license, and your sexual orientation becomes an issue, immediately retain a qualified attorney.

NOTES

1. A list of occupations subject to licensing restrictions was compiled
   in 1972 at the behest of the National Clearinghouse on Offender Employment Restrictions.
2. 129 U.S. 114, 122 (1889). Accord: Martin v. Walton, 368 U.S. 25
   (1961); Olsen v. Nebraska, 313 U.S. 236, 246 (1941); Graves v.
   Minnesota, 272 U.S. 425 (1926).
3. See, e.g. Note, *Due Process Limitations on Occupational Licensing*,
   59 Va. L. Rev. 1097 (1973).
4. Ironically, the courts have been somewhat less reluctant to strike
   down licensing restrictions relating to minimum "standards," particularly when the restriction has specified that the requisite level of skill
   to engage in an occupation may be obtained only in a specifically
   approved manner. See Note, *Entrance and Disciplinary Requirements for Occupational Licenses in California*, 14 Stan. L. Rev. 533,
   539–40 (1962).
5. 353 U.S. 232 (1957).
6. *Id*. at 238–39. See also Keyishian v. Board of Regents, 385 U.S. 589
   (1967); Cramp v. Board of Public Instruction, 368 U.S. 278 (1961);
   Green v. McElroy, 360 U.S. 474 (1959).
7. 1 Cal. 3d 214, 82 Cal. Rptr. 175, 461 P.2d 375 (1969).
8. 461 P.2d, at 382.
9. *Id*. at 394; citing Yakov v. Board of Medical Examiners, 68 Cal. 2d
   67, 75, 139 Cal. Rptr. 785, 791, 435 P.2d 553, 559 (1968).
10. 19 Cal. 3d 691, 139 Cal. Rptr. 700, 556 P.2d 602 (1977).
11. 33 N.Y. 2d 586, 347 N.Y.S. 2d 453 (1973).
12. 358 So. 2d 7 (Fla. 1978).
13. E.g. *Gaylord v. Tacoma School District, No. 10*, 88 Wash. 2d
    286, 559 P.2d 1340 (1977), *cert. denied*, 98 S. Ct. 234 (1977).

IV

The Armed Services

Vast numbers of gays have served honorably in the armed services in times of peace and war, and many gays are still in uniform. This central fact stands in stark contrast to official military pronouncements, and makes the exclusionary policies so vigorously pursued by the armed services all the more distressing and absurd.

The discussion that follows will examine the major pitfalls faced by gays in the military. Probably the most important lessons to be learned, are that gays need not sacrifice the constitutional rights enjoyed by all Americans during their military service, and that the assistance of a lawyer or other qualified person can help to ensure that those rights will be respected should sexual orientation become an issue.[1]

What is the official military policy regarding gays?

Regulations newly adopted by the Department of Defense state:

Homosexuality is incompatible with military service. The presence in the military environment of persons who engage in homosexual conduct or who, by their statements, demonstrate a propensity to engage in homosexual conduct, seriously impairs the accomplishment of the military mission. The presence of such members adversely affects the ability of the military services to maintain discipline, good order, and morale; to foster mutual trust and confidence among service members; to insure the integrity of the system of rank and command; to facilitate assignment and worldwide deployment of service members who frequently must live and work under close conditions affording minimal privacy; to recruit and retain members of the military services; to maintain the public acceptability of military service; and to prevent breaches of security.[2]

Thus, the Department requires the discharge of any service member who, prior to or during military service, (1) "engaged in, attempted to engage in, or solicited another to engage in a homosexual act"; (2) "has stated that he or she is a homosexual or bisexual," unless there is a finding that the individual is not a homosexual or bisexual; or (3) "has married or attempted to marry a person known to be of the same biological sex," unless there is a finding that the individual "is not a homosexual or bisexual and that the purpose of the marriage attempt was the avoidance or termination of military service."[3]

The new regulations permit one exception to the general rule of exclusion. A person may stay in the military, even though he or she has committed, or attempted to commit, a homosexual act, as long as the following conditions are met: if the act was a "departure from the member's usual and customary behavior," was done without "force, coercion, or intimidation," and is "unlikely to recur," if the member "does not desire to engage in or intend to engage in [further] homosexual acts," and if "the member's continued presence in the Service is deemed consistent with the interest of the Service in proper discipline, good order, and morale." Otherwise, he or she must be, as the department puts it, "separated" from service.[4]

What are the possible consequences of being identified as a homosexual by the military?

If an individual is identified as a homosexual by the military and does not fall within the narrow and rarely-used exception just described, he or she will usually be administratively discharged from the service. Military regulations provide for four characterizations of administrative discharge. The *Honorable* characterization is appropriate "when the quality of the member's service generally has met the standards of acceptable conduct and performance of duty for military personnel."[5] A *General* (under honorable conditions) discharge is granted when the "member's service has been honest and faithful," but "significant negative aspects of the member's conduct or performance of duty outweigh positive aspects of the member's military record."[6] A discharge *Under Other Than Honorable Conditions* (formerly called the *Undesirable* discharge) is imposed when the reason for separation is based upon one or more acts or omissions, or upon a pattern of behavior, that "constitute a significant departure from the conduct expected of members of the Military Services."[7] A discharge Under Other Than Honorable Conditions may not be imposed in separations for homosexuality unless there is also a finding that during the current term of service the member attempted, solicited, or committed a homosexual act under one or more of the following circumstances: by "using force, coercion, or intimidation;" "[w]ith a person under sixteen years of age;" "[w]ith a subordinate in circumstances that violate customary military superior-subordinate relationships;" "[o]penly in public view;" "[f]or compensation;" "[a]board a military vessel or aircraft;" *or* "[i]n another location subject to military control under aggravating circumstances . . . that have an adverse impact on discipline, good order, or morale comparable to the impact of such activity aboard a vessel or aircraft."[8] Finally, a discharge may be categorized as an *Entry Level Separation* without characterization if the member has not yet completed the first 180 days of continuous active duty service and neither an Honorable nor an Under Other Than Honorable Conditions characterization is clearly warranted under the circumstances.[9]

In addition to the various categories of administrative discharge, two types of punitive discharges may be imposed pursuant to court-martial conviction. *Bad Conduct* discharges may be given by either special or general court-martial, while the *Dishonorable* discharge, the most stigmatizing discharge inflicted by the military, can be given only by sentence of a general court martial.[10] Although court-martial proceedings are not often brought in response to charges of homosexuality, both active-duty[11] and retired[12] service members have occasionally been prosecuted by court-martial for homosexual conduct. Article 125 of the Uniform Code of Military Justice[13] proscribes sodomy, defined as "unnatural copulation with another person of the same or opposite sex or with an animal," and is punishable by Dishonorable discharge and up to five years confinement at hard labor, even in the absence of "aggravating" circumstances.[14] The general articles, prohibiting "conduct unbecoming an officer and a gentleman,"[15] and "all conduct of a nature to bring discredit upon the armed forces,"[16] may also be used to punish homosexual acts with Dishonorable discharge and imprisonment.[17]

In recent years, roughly sixty-seven percent of enlisted service members separated for homosexuality have received Honorable discharges, slightly more than twenty-eight percent have received General discharges (under honorable conditions), and approximately four percent have received discharges Under Other Than Honorable Conditions; no Bad Conduct or Dishonorable discharges have been reported.[18] Although these figures reflect improvement over times past when thousands of gay men and lesbians received Dishonorable discharges for homosexuality, they compare less favorably to discharge statistics for the general military population: over ninety percent of all enlisted separations are fully Honorable, between four percent and five percent are General (under honorable conditions), roughly three percent are Under Other Than Honorable Conditions, while well under one percent receive Bad Conduct or Dishonorable discharges.[19]

Have any courts found the military's policy of either excluding or discharging gays to be unconstitutional?

Several federal district courts have ruled against the military's exclusionary policy, on the grounds that it arbitrarily excludes homosexuals.[20]

But the only appellate court to have considered the issue directly held that this policy of excluding gays has a sufficiently rational basis to be within constitutional limits.[21]

Another federal appeals court ruled in 1978, that the policies of the air force and navy then in effect, were too vague.[22] In response, the Department of Defense revised its policy, resulting in the regulations set forth above. The validity of the department's new regulations has yet to be determined.

How many homosexuals are separated from the military each year?

In recent years over 1,700 people have been separated from the military annually for homosexuality.[23] This represents considerably less than one percent of the total number of people annually discharged from the military,[24] and probably something less than one percent of the total number of predominantly homosexual males serving in the military at any period.[25] At a minimum, it can be said that in dealing with its "homosexual problem" the military has not been remarkably successful. That fact provides scant solace, however, to the officer or enlisted person caught up in the web the military has created to deal with those involved in, suspected of, associated with, or inclined toward homosexuality.

What circumstances trigger an investigation of a serviceman or woman for homosexual involvement?

Most commonly, an investigation of an individual's sexual orientation is initiated because of a report from some source indicating that the individual has participated in a homosexual act, or that he or she has been arrested for a criminal offense related to sexual orientating or has homosexual "tendencies." Military psychiatrists have been known to submit such a report, while military chaplains are likely to suggest that the individual speak with someone having administrative authority over such matters. Often an individual's name surfaces in connection with another case: in conducting an investigation of a serviceman or woman suspected of homosexual involvement, military investigators invariably try to gain from the individual under investigation, information about the homosexual involvement of others. Sometimes servicemen and women volunteer such information. Finally, there are rare occasions in which the process begins because someone has been observed engaging in sexual relations with a person of the same sex.

At what point is the person suspected of homosexual involvement informed that an investigation is being conducted, or about to be initiated?

An informal investigation, including surveillance and questioning of friends and acquaintances, may progress for some time before the individual is informed that he or she is suspected of homosexual involvement. At the time a formal investigation is begun, the individual suspected of homosexual involvement, may be summoned to appear before a commanding officer or, more often, before the investigative agent involved in the case. The individual is informed that an investigation is being conducted and is given an often exaggerated indication of the adverse evidence already obtained. Sometimes, the individual is first informed in writing that an investigation is underway. Any security clearance probably will be suspended at this point.

If a person is called before a commanding officer or investigator, what rights are available?

During every stage of the process, beginning with initial questioning, an individual has certain basic rights, which include the following:

1. To be informed of the specific "offenses."
2. To remain silent.
3. To be informed that anything said may be used against him or her.
4. To have the advice and assistance of a lawyer or other qualified counsel, either an appointed military lawyer or civilian counsel retained at personal expense, and to consult with a lawyer prior to responding to charges.[26]

If after being informed of these rights, a person decides to waive one or more of them, can they be asserted later?

Not necessarily. But the best advice is not to waive them in the first place, particularly the right to consult with an attorney before doing anything else. In most circumstances, two heads are better than one—and seldom is this more true than when an investigation has been initiated by military authorities involving charges of homosexual activity. *Immediately upon being informed that you are under investigation, you should refuse to answer questions of any sort; and you should contact a lawyer or other qualified counsel!*

If for some reason you waive one or more of your rights at the outset of an investigation, you may nevertheless assert those rights later, but you will have the burden of showing that the previous waiver should be invalidated.

How are charges involving homosexuality generally investigated?

The most significant part of the investigative process is the personal interrogation conducted by investigative agents.[27] The interrogation may last several hours and stretch over several days. As recommended, if a lawyer hasn't been consulted, one should not submit to the interrogation at all. The investigators will try to convince you that you really don't have to see a lawyer prior to speaking with them; that they are hopeful that everything will be fine once you cooperate and are released from the service; that they will help get you medical assistance; that they already have all the information about you that they need, but would like to have you clarify a couple of "details"; that no one need know of the military's action if you cooperate; and that if you don't "cooperate" by confessing, the maximum penalty is likely to be imposed (that is, you will be referred for a trial by court-martial and be given a punitive discharge). Often, there will be two investigative agents present at the interrogation; one will try to gain your confidence as a good guy, and the other will play the role of the bad guy. They may try to get you to take a lie-detector test. *You should refuse*.

In short, while the investigative agents are obligated to inform you of your rights, they will do their level best to convince you that you have no option other than "confessing" to the charges and otherwise cooperating with them. In fact, you have other options. Do not cooperate; insist on seeing a lawyer instead.

Charges are often brought on the scantiest of evidence. Thus, the interrogation by investigative agents is often the crucial factor in the process. The facts you disclose at that point, may be of pivotal importance in determining whether the charges against you are dismissed or pursued.

The investigators, even without your permission, may search your personal belongings for incriminating evidence (magazines, letters, advertisements, pictures, address books, and so forth). You should not consent to such a search—even if the agents produce a warrant—but should insist on seeing a lawyer. As a general rule, you should be careful that your personal belongings stored on base, do not contain anything that could incriminate you or anyone else.

Once you have confessed, there may be little a lawyer can

do to help you. But if your confession was obtained before you were informed of your rights, an attorney can help to ensure that it is not used against you if the case proceeds to trial by court-martial. Whether such a confession can be used against you in an administrative proceeding leading to discharge under other than honorable conditions, has not yet been definitively resolved.[28] You should nevertheless contact a lawyer even if you have signed a confession.

If referred to a psychiatrist, will any statements made to him be kept confidential?

No. Military law does not recognize the principle of privileged communications in relationships between military doctors and patients.[29] Referral of an individual suspected of homosexual involvement to a psychiatrist (or to a medical officer if no psychiatrist is available), for a professional evaluation, is an important step in the investigative process. It is not intended to "help" you. Any statements you make to the psychiatrist (or medical officer) that tend to support the conclusion that you are an overt homosexual or possess homosexual tendencies, will find their way into the psychiatrist's report. The psychiatrist or medical officer also may conclude that you need medical attention and may recommend separation under medical regulations. Depending on the type of information contained in the report, you may or may not be given a copy. A copy definitely will be forwarded to those in charge of the investigation, however, and a copy will be included in your permanent record.

What happens once the investigation has been completed?

Once the investigation has been completed, you will be informed that (1) the evidence did not support the charges that had been made, and that the charges were consequently dropped, or (2) the charge has been referred for trial by general or special court-martial, or (3) an administrative discharge appears to be warranted, and that you have a right to appear before a board of officers,[30] but that you may waive that step and agree to accept an administrative discharge.

You should not waive your right to an administrative board without first consulting with a lawyer.

What rights would one have before the board of officers?

You may testify on your own behalf (although you cannot be compelled to do so), question the witnesses appearing against you, call witnesses on your own behalf, and introduce other evidence in your favor.[31] But you should bear in mind that the board cannot compel civilians to appear as witnesses; thus, you may not be able to confront and cross-examine persons who have submitted affidavits or other documents containing adverse information.[32] Again, you have the right to be represented by an attorney during your appearance before the board of officers, and you should exercise that right.[33]

What procedure is followed if the board of officers recommend discharge from the military, or if a discharge is agreed to?

The record of the administrative proceedings will be turned over to a designated officer—the "Separation Authority"—for review. The Separation Authority has several options at that point. He or she may accede to the recommended discharge, direct that the recommended type of discharge be entered on your permanent record, and have your discharge papers signed. If the Separation Authority concludes that the recommended action is too severe, he may retain the member, upgrade the discharge recommended by the board of officers. The Separation Authority may not, however, give you a less favorable type of discharge than that recommended by the board of officers, or refer the case to a new board. Finally, the Separation Authority may initiate a further review of your case if he or she concludes there are grounds for doing so.[34]

The Separation Authority may not give you a less favorable type of discharge than that recommended by the board of officers.[35] However, if the board recommends retention, the Separation Authority may nevertheless forward the matter to the Secretary of the service branch with a recommendation for separation based on the circumstances of the case. The Secretary may then direct either separation or retention, but if separation is approved, the characterization of service cannot be less than a General discharge.[36]

What are the consequences of receiving a discharge less than fully honorable?

Because more than ninety percent of those servicemen and

women who leave the military receive Honorable discharges, a certain stigma attaches to all other types of discharges. Recipients of less than Honorable discharges, and even those honorably discharged whose term of service is cut short through administrative separation, often encounter difficulty in securing civilian employment. At a minimum, separation from the military because of homosexual involvement of some sort, may bar you from holding some federal and state jobs, particularly when a government-issued security clearance is a prerequisite. You also may be barred from holding a job in private industry that involves access to classified information.[37]

In addition to these employment disabilities, recipients of "Other Than Honorable Conditions discharges forfeit their rights to receive a salary for accrued leave,[38] to be buried in a national cemetery,[39] and to retain uniforms, ribbons, medals, or service bars.[40] Numerous other service-related benefits accrued during the current term of service—such as educational benefits, pensions for disabilities, vocational rehabilitation, loans, special housing, hospitalization, outpatient medical or dental treatment, and compensation for service-connected injuries or disabilities—are available to the recipient of discharge under Other Than Honorable Conditions only if extension of the benefit is approved by the administering agency, usually the Veterans' Administration (VA). Many recipients of an "Other Than Honorable Conditions discharge have been denied these benefits.[41]

The VA has, however, recently amended its "character of discharge" regulations to provide that only in certain aggravated cases will an other-than-honorable discharge on the grounds of homosexuality, be considered to have been issued under dishonorable conditions. Such aggravated cases would include child molestation, homosexual prostitution, homosexual acts accompanied by assault or coercion, or homosexual acts between service members of different rank where a person has taken advantage of his or her superior rank.

In virtually all other situations, the effect of the change in regulations is to make most persons discharged under other than honorable conditions for homosexuality, eligible for VA benefits.[42]

Once a person is separated administratively from the military on the basis of homosexual involvement, is there any chance that the discharge could be upgraded?

Yes. The prospect of a postseparation upgrading is often offered by military authorities (particularly investigative agents) as a reason why you should fully cooperate in the investigative process, and why you should agree to accept a less than fully honorable discharge. But the prospect of a later upgrade should not by itself induce you to accept a discharge of a lower level than your service record entitles you. The prospects of upgrading an administrative discharge are improving.[43] Since 1978, the military services have generally been willing to upgrade discharges to honorable, where the sole reason for the discharge was homosexuality, and where there are no aggravating circumstances. Before applying for a review of your discharge, you should seek the assistance of a lawyer or other qualified person.

What procedures are available for postseparation review of an administrative discharge?

Two relatively distinct administrative bodies have been created to review administrative discharges. The Discharge Review Board (DRB) of the service involved, has the authority to review administrative discharges on its own initiative, although it almost never does so; cases almost always are brought before the DRB's by the individual who has been discharged.[44] The DRB's may review and upgrade a discharge, or issue a new discharge,[45] but they cannot revoke a discharge, order reinstatement, or grant back pay. If the former serviceman or woman requests a hearing, the DRB's are obligated to grant that request.[46] DRB decisions to upgrade a discharge are subject to review by the secretary of the service branch involved.

Each branch of the military also has a Board for the Correction of Military Records (BCMR), staffed by civilians, which handles "appeals" from decisions made by the DRB's and also deals with demands for reinstatement and back pay.[47] In the past, however, the BCMR's have very rarely acted favorably on demands for reinstatement or back pay. Hearings before the BCMR's are discretionary and are rarely granted—but full relief may be granted without a hearing. If a hearing is granted, the procedures utilized by the BCMR's closely resemble those utilized by the DRB's.

Can I appeal from a conviction after trial by court-martial, or from an adverse decision by a DRB or a BCMR?

Yes. Every general or special court-martial resulting in a punitive (Bad Conduct or Dishonorable) discharge is automatically referred to a Court of Military Review[48], and may in some instances be further reviewed by the Court of Military Appeals.[49] On the completion of a military appellate review, some court-martial convictions also may be challenged in the federal courts.[50]

Administrative discharges can be reviewed in the federal courts[51] on four grounds: (1) failure of the particular service to follow its own procedural regulations, (2) absence of statutory authority to discharge, (3) failure to accord constitutional due process protections and (4) the arbitrary and capricous nature of the decision.[51] Most successful challenges to administrative discharges have been based on the first ground.[52]

Perhaps the primary thing to guard against while serving in the military, is being a party to your own undoing: the sad fact is that most servicemen and women charged with homosexual involvement, convict themselves by succumbing to the inducements and threats that confront them at every stage of the process leading to their discharge. If charges are lodged against you during your military service, you should consider very carefully the following:

1. *You should never attempt to go it alone*. Secure the assistance of a lawyer as soon as possible after being informed that charges have been made against you. If you cannot afford to hire a lawyer, ask that a lawyer be appointed to represent you. Do not make any statements or cooperate in any way until you have had an opportunity to consult with counsel.

2. *You do not sacrifice your constitutional rights while serving in the military*. Those rights were designed to protect you. Exercise them. You should not waive any of your rights before having consulted with counsel. Insist that you be given a written list of all the charges against you, and demand access to all relevant evidence.

3. *Do not accept the advice of military authorities regarding the consequences of any of the options available to you*. From the beginning of the administrative process leading to your discharge, you will be pressured into "cooperating." The

pressure will take many forms. You will be told, for example, that you will be dealt with more leniently if you confess and accept an undesirable discharge. You may also be told that once you become a civilian, you will stand a good chance of getting your discharge upgraded. Get counsel first. Then try to identify your options and determine how to proceed.

4. *Do not accept a less than Honorable discharge as the best option available to you*. You should insist on being given the discharge warranted by your service record. If you have an impressive service record, insist that you be given an Honorable discharge. Otherwise, insist on a General discharge. [53]

NOTES

1. For a more complete discussion of many of the issues discussed in this chapter, see Addlestone, Newman & Gross, *The Rights of Veterans* (Avon Books 1978), and Rivkin, *The Rights of Servicemen* (Avon Books 1973).

2. Enlisted Administrative Separations, Appendix A, Part 1, §H, 47 Fed. Reg. 10,162, 10,179 (1982) (to be codified at 32 C.F.R. Part 41) (effective October 1, 1982). These new regulations repeat nearly verbatim the Defense Department policy enunciated in January, 1981 (see 32 C.F.R. §41.13 1981).

3. Enlisted Administrative Separations, *supra* note 2. For the regulations promulgated by the various service branches implementing the new Defense Department regulation, see Army Regulations 635–100 and 635–212; Air Force Manual 39–12; Secretary of Navy Instruction 1900.9c; and Marine Corps Separation and Retirement Manual §§6016–6018. Most of the discussion in the text refers to separations of enlisted personnel. Officers may not be dismissed from the military except as a result of a general court-martial or by order of the President under limited circumstances. See 10 U.S.C. §1161 (1976). The consequences of a court-martial conviction are even more severe than the receipt of an administrative discharge. Officers charged with offenses related to homosexuality should, therefore, immediately consult with an attorney.

4. Enlisted Administrative Separations, *supra* note 2.

5. *Id*.

6. *Id*., Appendix A, Part 3, §C1b[2], 47 Fed. Reg. at 10, 183.

7. *Id*., Appendix A, Part 2, §C1b[3], (a) *1–2*, 47 Fed. Reg. at 10, 183.

8. *Id*., Appendix A, Part 1, §H2 a–g, 47 Fed. Reg. at 10, 179.

9. *Id.*, Appendix A, Part 3, §C3[1](a)–(b), 47 Fed. Reg. at 10, 183; *id.*, §41.6 (i), 47 Fed. Reg. at 10, 175.

10. See 10 U.S.C. §§818, 819 (Articles 18, 19, U.C.M.J). For the stigmatizing effects of bad conduct and dishonorable discharges, see Zillman et al., *The Military In American Society* §5.01 [1] (1978).

11. See, e.g. Hatheway v. Secretary of Army, 641 F. 2d 1376 (9th Cir. 1981).

12. See, e.g., Hooper v. United States, 326 F.2d 982 (Ct.Cl.), *cert. denied*, 377 U.S. 977 (1964).

13. 10 U.S.C. §925.

14. See "Table of Maximum Punishments," *Manual for Courts-Martial, United States, 1969* 25–14 (Executive Order No. 11,476) (revised 1980, Executive Order No. 12,198). When accompanied by force and without consent, sodomy is punishable by 10 years confinement at hard labor, and when the act involves a child under 16 years of age, confinement may be as high as 20 years.

15. 10 U.S.C. §933 (Art. 133, U.C.M.J.).

16. 10 U.S.C. §934 (Art. 134, U.C.M.J.).

17. See "Table of Maximum Punishments," *supra* note 14.

18. Information provided by Department of Defense in response to inquiry by U.S. Representative Theodore S. Weiss (New York). Of 1,738 enlisted separations for homosexuality in fiscal year 1980, 1,175 were Honorable, 494 were General, and 69 were Under Other Than Honorable Conditions. Preliminary, unaudited figures for fiscal year 1981 show that out of 1,742 discharges for homosexuality, 1,172 were Honorable, 500 were General, and 70 were Under Other Than Honorable Conditions. *Id.*

19. *Id.*

20. See, e.g., benShalom v. Sec'y of Army, 489 F. Supp. 964 (E.D. Wis. 1980); Martinez v. Brown, 449 F. Supp. 207 (N.D. Cal. 1978), *rev'd*, Beller v. Middendorf, 632 F.2d 788 (9th Cir. 1980), *cert. denied*, 102 S. Ct. 304 (1981); Saal v. Middendorf, 427 F. Supp. 192 (N.D. Cal. 1977) *rev'd sub nom.* Beller v. Middendorf, 632 F.2d 788 (9th Cir. 1980), *cert. denied*, 102 S. Ct. 304 (1981). For a particularly articulate exposition of the arguments against the constitutionality of the military's policy, see Miller v. Rumsfeld, 647 F.2d 80 (Norris, J., dissenting to denial of rehearing en banc in Beller v. Middendorf).

21. Beller v. Middendorf, 632 F.2d 788 (9th Cir. 1980) *cert. denied*, 102 S. Ct. 304 (1981).

22. Berg v. Claytor, 591 F.2d 849 (D.C. Cir. 1978), *rev'g* Berg v. Claytor, 436 F.Supp. 76 (D.D.C. 1977); Matlovich v. Secretary of the Air Force, 591 F.2d 852 (D.C. Cir. 1978).

23. Information provided by Department of Defense in response to inquiry by Representative Theodore S. Weiss (New York). This data indicated 1,738 enlisted separations for homosexuality in fiscal year 1980; preliminary unaudited figures for fiscal year 1981 indicate

1,742 enlisted separations for homosexuality. These figures do not reflect the discharges of gays who, after being identified by the military as homosexuals, are discharged under general charges of "unsuitability," "unfitness," or "misconduct", as opposed to specific charges of homosexuality.

24. In 1980, a total of 541,558 enlisted personnel were discharged from the military; for 1981, the figure was 530,718. Information provided by Department of Defense in response to inquiry by Representative Theodore S. Weiss (New York).

25. In 1980, military strength totalled 2,031,658, down from a total of 3,059,837 in 1970. See *The World Almanac and Book of Facts 1982* (H. Lane, ed. 1982), 329–31. Fewer than 11.3 percent of these totals are women. *Id.* at 331. If the Kinsey estimate that at least ten percent of the male population is predominantly homosexual is applied to the remaining male military population, then more than 180,000 gay men should have been serving in the military in 1980, and over 271,000 gay men would have been in the armed forces in 1970.

26. See generally 10 U.S.C. §831 (Art. 31, U.C.M.J.); for an analysis of Article 31, see Lederer, *Rights Warnings In The Armed Services*, 72 Mil. L. Rev. 1 (1976). Whether information obtained in the absence of rights warnings is admissible in administrative discharge hearings, as opposed to courts-martial, is subject to question. See note 28, *infra*.

27. Depending on the service, the investigative agent would be from the Criminal Investigation Division (C.I.D.) of the Army, the Naval Investigative Service (N.I.S.) of the Navy, or the Office of Special Investigations (O.S.I.) of the Air Force.

28. In a recent case, the United States Court of Appeals for the District of Columbia Circuit ruled that evidence obtained through mandatory urinanalysis was compulsory self-incrimination and was inadmissible not only in court-martial proceedings but also in administrative discharge proceedings in which a less than full honorable discharge might be imposed. See Giles v. Secretary of the Army, 627 F.2d 554 (1980), *aff'g and modifying on other grounds*, 475 F. Supp. 595 (1979). Thus, although the extent to which the rules of evidence protect a servicemember in administrative discharge hearings is still unresolved, it seems clear that at least *some* protection is afforded.

29. See *Manual for Courts-Martial, United States, 1969*, 27–38 (Executive Order No. 11,476) (revised 1980, Executive Order No. 12,198) (Military R. Evid. 501 (d)).

30. Ordinarily, enlisted servicemembers are entitled to administrative board hearings only if the member has six or more years of total military service or if the discharge characterization is Under Other Than Honorable Conditions. See Enlisted Administrative Separations, Appendix A, Part 2, §C2b[3](b), 47 Fed. Reg. 10,162, 10,183

(1982) (to be codified at 32 C.F.R. Part 41) (effective October 1, 1982); *id.*, Appendix A, Part 3, §Blg, 47 Fed. Reg. at 10,184. However, the new regulations appear to require administrative board action in all cases of separation for homosexuality, unless the right to a board is waived. *Id.*, Appendix A, Part 1, §H3, 47 Fed. Reg. at 10,179.

31. *Id.*, Appendix A, Part 3, §C5f, 47 Fed. Reg. at 10,186.

32. See *id.*, Appendix A, Part 3, §C5c, 47 Fed. Reg. at 10,186.

33. For a general discussion of your rights before the board of officers, see Lunding, "Judicial Review of Military Administrative Discharges," 83 Yale L.J. 33, 38–40 (1973).

34. Enlisted Administrative Separations, Appendix A, Part 3, §C6d, 47 Fed. Reg. at 10,187; *id.*, Appendkx A, Part 1, §H3d, 47 Fed. Reg. at 10,179.

35. *Id.*, Appendix A, Part 3, §C6d[3][b]2, 47 Fed. Reg. at 10,187.

36. *Id.*, Appendix A, Part 1, §H3d[1][b], 47 Fed. Reg. at 10,179.

37. *Id.*, Appendix A, Part 3, §C6d[2][b], 47 Fed. Reg. at 10,187. For a discussion of the general difficulties encountered by those receiving stigmatizing discharges, see generally Jones, *The Gravity of Administrative Discharges: A Legal And Empirical Evaluation,* 59 Mil. L. Rev. 1 (1973); Lunding, *Judicial Review of Military Administrative Discharges,* 83 Yale L.J. 33, 33–36 (1973). For a discussion of difficulties in obtaining security clearances, see Chapter V of this book.

38. 37 U.S.C. §501(e).

39. 32 C.F.R. §553,17(b)(1981)(Army-operated national cemetaries). Recipients of discharges Under Other Than Honorable Conditions may be eligible for burial in national cemetaries operated by the Veterans Administration, however. See 38 C.F.R. §1.621(a)(1981).

40. 10 U.S.C. §771a(b); see also 32 C.F.R. §578.3(k) (1981)(Army regulation on ribbons and decorations).

41. Federal law defines a "veteran" as a person discharged from military service "under conditions other than dishonorable," 38 U.S.C. §101(2), and vests the Veterans Administration with broad discretion for determining eligibility for veterans' benefits. See 38 U.S.C. §§210 (c)(1), 3103(e)(1). Prior to 1980, the Veterans Administration considered any Undesirable discharge (the name formerly used for discharges Under Other Than Honorable Conditions) received for homosexual acts to have been issued under dishonorable conditions. See 38 C.F.R. §3.12d(1979); Jones, *The Gravity of Administrative Discharges: A Legal And Empirical Evaluation, supra* note 37, 11–12 (1973). Thus, under the former regulations, an individual with an Undesirable discharge for homosexuality was not a "veteran" and was ineligible for veterans' benefits.

42. Veterans-Discharge, Veterans Administration Rules and Regs. Amended January 1, 1980. 48 U.S.L.W. 2480 (Jan. 22, 1980). See 38 C.F.R. §3.12 (d)(5)(1981).

43. See Addlestone, et al., *The Rights of Veterans*, 86–87 (1978).

44. Use DoD Form 293 for this purpose. Such forms are available at any Veterans Administration Office. Request for review must be made within 15 years of the date of discharge. 10 U.S.C. §1553(a).

45. See 10 U.S.C. §1553; 32 C.F.R. §70.5(d)(4)(iii)(1981).

46. 32 C.F.R. §70.5(b)(3)(1981).

47. See 10 U.S.C. §1552; Knehans v. Alexander, 566 F.2d 312 (D.C. Cir. 1977), *cert. denied*, 435 U.S. 995 (1978). Application for review by the BCMR must be made within three years of the discovery of error or injustice in the service record, although exceptions may be made "in the interest of justice," 10 U.S.C. §1552(b). Use DoD Form 149 to request review of your record by the BCMR, which may be obtained at any Veterans Administration office.

48. 10 U.S.C. §866(b) (Art. 66, U.C.M.J.).

49. 10 U.S.C. §867(b)–(a) (Art. 67, U.C.M.J.).

50. See generally H. Moyer, *Justice and the Military*, Ch. 6 (1973).

51. This includes the Court of Claims, which has now been empowered to order both reinstatement and back pay and which in several recent cases has shown some willingness to correct abuses by the military in this area. See generally Glosser & Rosenberg, *Military Correction Boards: Administrative Process and Review by the United States Court of Claims*, 23 Am. U.L. Rev. 391, 409–24 (1973).

51. See Lunding, *Judicial Review of Military Administrative Discharges*, *supra* note 37, 42–58 (1973). Administrative discharge boards are not required to follow all of the procedures that are observed in a judicial hearing. The Fifth and Sixth Amendment rights of confrontation and cross-examination, for example, have not been established as absolute constitutional requirements in board hearings. See Pickell v. Reed, 326 F. Supp. 1086, 1090 (N.D.Cal.), *aff'd on other grounds*, 446 F.2d 898 (9th Cir.), *cert. denied*, 404 U.S. 946 (1971); Jones, *The Gravity of Administrative Discharges: A Legal And Empirical Evaluation*, *supra* note 37, 1–10 (1973).

52. See e.g. discussion and authorities cited in Lunding, *Judicial Review of Military Administrative Discharges*, *supra* note 37, 42–73 (1973). See also, Berg v. Claytor, and Matlovich v. Secretary of the Air Force *supra* note 22.

53. The authors gratefully acknowledge the invaluable assistance and advice of Sherry Michaelson, a student at New York University School of Law, in the preparation of this chapter.

V

Security Clearances

The problems that confront gays in their efforts to secure suitable employment, increase significantly whenever the particular job at stake has been deemed for any reason, to be unusually sensitive. The jobs from which professed gays have been most uniformly excluded—and with respect to which administrative and judicial challenges have been least successful, until very recently—have been those involving access to governmentally classified information.

The federal government's present policy of requiring security clearances on a wide range of jobs, and of denying clearances to known or suspected homosexuals, has its roots in the post-World War II period. Prior to that time, neither the federal government (except the military branches), nor private employers, routinely inquired into the sexual orientation of their employees. As a consequence, the freedom of at least those gays who were scrupulously discreet about their private sexual lives to pursue nonmilitary occupations, appears to have been relatively unencumbered.

In the anti-Communist hysteria of the late 1940s and 1950s, the situation changed dramatically. Claiming that they were acting to protect national security, those in positions of authority embarked, during the cold war period, on a concerted campaign to exclude gays from important jobs in the federal government. That campaign has continued to the present, although there are encouraging signs that this situation is changing.

Are all employees of the federal government required to have a government-issued security clearance?

No. Only federal employees who occupy "sensitive" positions must possess a security clearance. A "sensitive" position is defined in Executive Order No. 10450, as amended, to encompass "any position . . . the occupant of which could bring about, by virtue of the nature of the position, a material adverse effect on the national security. . . ."[1] The heads of all federal departments and agencies must ensure that all permanent occupants of those positions possess a security clearance.

How is the security-clearance program for federal employees administered?

Several federal departments and agencies—such as the Department of Defense, the State Department, and the Federal Bureau of Investigation—have their own security-clearance programs. But, most federal departments and agencies rely on the Civil Service Commission to conduct security investigations, and to issue security clearances to employees occupying "sensitive" positions.

Have gays been able to secure and retain security clearances?

As one would expect, gays are employed at all levels of the federal bureaucracy and in positions classified as "sensitive," as well as "nonsensitive." Thousands of gays undoubtedly hold federal security clearances, some for many years. However, the key to the initial and continued employment of such persons has been discretion. Mere suspicion that an applicant for, or a holder of, a security clearance is gay, or has in the past engaged in homosexual activity, has often been enough to endanger access to classified material. Actual proof of homosexual activity has typically resulted in the denial of applications for security clearances, as well as the revocation of clearances already held.

This practice may be changing. In several recent incidents, the government has permitted certain *non*government workers to obtain or keep their security clearances. (Nongovernment workers sometimes need security clearances if they work for employers who are under contract with the Department of Defense or one of the armed services.) This suggests that the federal government is altering this general attitude on the issue of whether gays can have security clearances, whether they work for the federal government or for a company under contract to the government. This development is described in greater detail below.

What is the legal basis for the denial of a security clearance?
Federal departments and agencies are directed by executive orders, to deny applications for security clearances unless employment of the particular individual being investigated "is clearly consistent with the interests of the national security." To this end, administrators of the various federal employees security programs are instructed by Executive Order No. 10450, to gather information relating, among other things, to the following:

(i) Any behavior, activities, or associations which tend to show that the individual is not reliable or trustworthy.

(ii) Any deliberate misrepresentations, falsifications, or omissions of material facts.

(iii) Any criminal, infamous, dishonest, immoral, or notoriously disgraceful conduct, habitual use of intoxicants to excess, drug addiction, sexual perversion, or financial irresponsibility.

(iv) Any illness, including any mental condition, of a nature which in the opinion of competent medical authority may cause significant defect in the judgment or reliability of the employee, with due regard to the transient or continuing effect of the illness and the medical findings in such case.[2]

Each case is supposed to be determined individually, but until very recently, knowledge, or even suspicion, of an applicant's homosexuality, inevitably resulted in a denial of clearance.

How does evidence of homosexuality normally come to the attention of security investigators?
Applicants for federal jobs requiring security clearances, must reveal detailed information about their activities on appropriate forms. In the case of federal civil service jobs, applicants are required to fill out Standard Form 171 and

Standard Form 78. Question 23C of Standard Form 171 asks whether the applicant has ever been discharged from the military under other than honorable conditions. Question 29 asks whether the applicant has ever been convicted of breaking the law, has ever forfeited collateral, or is presently subject to a criminal proceeding. Standard Form 78, which is concerned primarily with the applicant's medical condition, inquires among other things, into whether the applicant has ever been hospitalized or treated for a mental illness. The applicant's answers to these questions could of course provide a predicate for a more direct and detailed inquiry into whether the applicant has ever engaged in homosexual conduct.

In addition, the Civil Service Commission and others responsible for monitoring the access of federal employees to classified information almost always check arrest and court records and the files of other state and federal agencies—including those maintained by the FBI. This is supplemented by personal interviews with both the applicant, and his acquaintances; direct questions may be asked about homosexual conduct, if any of the answers give rise to suspicion.

Evidence of homosexual conduct in employees already possessing a security clearance, often arises in connection with an updating or upgrading of the clearance. The investigation conducted in those circumstances closely resembles the investigation conducted on an initial application, and may be initiated after a reported arrest, or after one has been observed in places known to be frequented by gays.

Is a security clearance a prerequisite to certain jobs only with the federal government?

No. The earliest program requiring security clearances was designed to prevent the unauthorized disclosure of government-classified material by the employees of private companies performing work for the government.[3] The Supreme Court held in *Green* v. *McElroy* in 1959, that this program had not been sufficiently authorized.[4]

President Eisenhower responded to *Green* v. *McElroy* by issuing an executive order specifically authorizing the Department of Defense to create a program restricting the release of classified information in the private sector to those who had applied for, and received, a security clearance.[5] In its present form, the program covers various industries engaged in defense-related research and manufacturing activities. Approximately 2.2 million workers in private industry are subject to industrial security-clearance procedures.

How is the present industrial security program administered?

The initial processing of security-clearance requests, as well as requests for an upgrading or updating of current clearances, is done by the Defense Industrial Security Clearance Office (DISCO) in Columbus, Ohio.[6] If DISCO approves the application, the employer and employee are notified, and the matter ends. But if DISCO is unable to make a determination, it will contact the Industrial Security Clearance Review Office (ISCRO) in Washington, D.C., for a final decision.

Have gays been able to secure and retain industrial security clearances?

Again, the answer is yes, but until the late 1970s, discretion was essential. The administrators of the industrial security-clearance program—like those responsible for the security programs governing federal employees—would generally pay lip service to the notion that individual circumstances are taken into account. In fact, the opposite appeared to be true in cases in which there was evidence that the applicant or employee was gay.

Since approximately 1978, there has been a noticeable shift in the government's attitude. In several reported cases, gays have been able to obtain and keep industrial security clearances.

In 1977, for example, a man employed by a company in New York State that supplied electronic equipment to the Department of Defense was arrested at the U.S.-Canadian border while returning from a Canadian vacation for the unauthorized possession of amphetamines. The arrest triggered a general investigation by DISCO, and the investigation uncovered that the worker was gay and occasionally smoked marijuana. DISCO revoked his clearance. The worker appealed, and DISCO's decision was overturned. Crucial to the successful appeal was testimony by the worker that he was openly gay and therefore not subject to blackmail.[7]

Similarly, a worker at an electronics plant near San Francisco brought suit against the army in 1980 because it had rescinded, on the grounds of homosexuality, a clearance he had held for twelve years. Shortly after institution of the suit, the Army agreed to settle, admitting that the revocation had been in error. Significantly, in the settlement agreement the Army acknowledged the general principle that a clearance should not be denied or revoked solely because an applicant had engaged in homosexual conduct if that conduct was "private," "publicly acknowledged," and "legal in the state or other jurisdiction in which it occurs."[8]

What are the significant steps in the processing of a security clearance?

We have already discussed how security investigations are generally initiated. The procedures followed from that point differ rather substantially from program to program, although the procedures employed in processing industrial security clearances, are not atypical.

The security forms filled out at an early stage of the industrial security-clearance process, are sent to DISCO in Columbus, Ohio, for an initial review. If because of an adverse recommendation by DISCO, the application is referred to ISCRO in Washington, D.C., the matter is either assigned to the ISCRO Screening Board, or returned to DISCO for further consideration.

If assigned to the screening board, a further investigation by one of the security divisions of the three branches of the military is sometimes conducted; the applicant is often required to respond to written questions. Interviews with the applicant and his or her acquaintances are also required. A decision is then made by the screening board, and a Statement of Reasons is issued if that decision is unfavorable to the applicant.

The applicant is then afforded an opportunity to file a written reply to the charges made and he may request a hearing. The applicant may be accompanied by counsel before the hearing examiner, and he may introduce evidence and present witnesses on his own behalf, and may cross-examine witnesses against him.

If the examiner rules against the applicant, the decision may be appealed to the Appeal Board, which rules exclusively upon the written record as transmitted to it by the hearing examiner. If the Appeal Board sustains the prior decisions to revoke or deny a security clearance, the applicant's only remaining recourse is the courts.

It is not unusual for several years to elapse between the filing of the initial application, and the issuance of a final decision.[9]

Is access permitted to classified information during that time?

If you do not have an outstanding security clearance, the answer is almost invariably no; rarely, if ever, are "temporary" clearances granted during the pendency of the review process. If your employer performs little but government-related contract work, you may not be able to work for that employer until the application for a security clearance is granted. If you already have a security clearance, you generally will be permitted to continue to hold that clearance during the review process. That will depend, however, on the seriousness of the reservations motivating DISCO to recommend against continuing the clearance, and on the extent of your willingness to "cooperate" with those conducting the investigation.

How have challenges to the denial of security clearances to gays and others who have engaged in isolated instances of homosexual conduct, fared in court?

Until the 1980 case against the army described on p. 53, court decisions on this issue almost invariably favored the government. In *Adams* v. *Laird*,[10] for example, the United States Court of Appeals for the District of Columbia, affirmed a lower court decision in favor of the government without any real evidence that the applicant was a security risk—other than evidence tending to show that the applicant had at times engaged in homosexual activity. The applicant had held a *Secret* security clearance for approximately eight years without any misuse of classified material. The investigation that ultimately led to the revocation of the applicant's *Secret* clearance, began when he applied for a *Top Secret* clearance.

A point that may have weighed against the applicant in *Adams* v. *Laird*, was that he had apparently admitted during the course of an interrogation that he had engaged in homosexual activity. Later, he refused to admit that such conduct had occurred, and argued that the circumstances attending the interrogation had been so coercive, as to void his admissions. The court rejected the argument that the interrogation had been unfairly coercive, and noted as well, that the applicant's subsequent denials "hardly cast . . . him in the role of the avowed but aggrieved homosexual who insists that his qualifications to maintain security are no less than those of anyone else."

In three 1973 cases involving the revocation of industrial security clearances,[11] the Court of Appeals for the District of Columbia again ruled against the applicants who were avowed gays, even though there was no evidence that any of them had ever abused classified information.

If a question is raised regarding a current clearance on grounds of homosexual conduct, what should be done?

If you plan to apply for a security clearance, the first thing you should do is contact a lawyer or a group with experience in such matters. Another good starting point would be to contact a gay organization, if one exists in your area.[12] If you already hold a security clearance and a question is raised concerning your sexual orientation, do not respond to any inquiry—no matter how innocuous or innocent it may appear—prior to consulting with counsel.

If the issue is ever raised, should sexual orientation be hidden or lied about?

Do not lie. Unless the issue of your sexual conduct or orientation is raised by someone else, you probably should not volunteer that information. On the other hand, you should never try to answer a question inaccurately in the course of a security investigation. Questions should be answered truthfully, or not answered at all.

NOTES

1. 18 Fed. Reg. 2489 (1953), as amended by Executive Order 11785, 3 C.F.R. 874 (1975).
2. The grounds that are sometimes used to deny gays industrial security clearances, see discussion *infra*, are set forth in Department of Defense Directive No. 5220.6, as amended.

3. The express functions of this early program were "to deny clearance for employment on aeronautical or classified contract work when such consent was required, and to suspend individuals, whose continued employment was considered inimical to the security interests of the United States, from employment on classified work." Committee on Government Security, S. Doc. No. 64, 85th Cong., 1st sess. (1957), 239.

4. Green v. McElroy, 360 U.S. 474 (1959).

5. Executive Order No. 10,865, 25 Fed. Reg. 1583 (1960), *as amended*, 32 C.F.R. §155 *et seq*. Such a program was actually set up by Department of Defense Directive No. 5220.6 VII B., E., F., H. (1966).

6. The procedures for updating and upgrading clearances are essentially the same as those for originally obtaining a clearance.

7. Reported in *N.Y. Civil Liberties*, the newsletter of the New York Civil Liberties Union, Jan.-Feb. 1979, 3.

8. Preston v. Brown, C–80–0994 (N.D. Cal.), Settlement Agreement dated Nov. 10, 1980. The settlement was reported in *The New York Times*, Nov. 16, 1980.

9. For a more detailed explanation of present industrial security clearance procedures, see Note, *Security Clearance for Homosexuals*, 25 Stan. L. Rev. 403, 406, *et seq*. (1973).

10. 420 F.2d 230 (1969), *cert. denied*, 397 U.S. 1039 (1970).

11. Gayer v. Schlesinger, Ulrich v. Schlesinger, and Wentworth v. Schlesinger, 490 F.2d 740 (1973), *as amended*, 494 F.2d 1135 (1974).

12. A list of such organizations is included in Appendix E.

VI

Immigration and Naturalization

May aliens be excluded from the United States because they have engaged in homosexual conduct?

Generally yes. Section 212 of the Immigration and Nationality Act[1] provides that aliens who are "afflicted with psychopathic personality, or sexual deviation, or a mental defect," are ineligible to receive a visa or to enter the United States. It also excludes aliens who admit having committed a crime involving "moral turpitude," or who have been convicted of such a crime. The phrases "psychopathic personality" and "sexual deviation" have complex legal histories, and arguments could be drawn from those histories to prevent their application to many persons who have engaged in homosexual conduct, but have committed no crime. The controlling fact is, however, that the Supreme Court held in 1967, in *Boutilier* v. *Immigration and Naturalization Service*,[2] that an alien may be excludable as having a "psychopathic personality," if he or she is, at the time of attempted entry into the United States, a "homosexual."

Since *Boutilier*, of course, there has been a momentous change in attitudes toward homosexuality, both in the medical community, and in the society at large. For instance, the American Psychiatric Association no longer classifies homosexuality as a psychological disorder. But these recent developments have yet to prompt a reform of the immigration laws, or to convince courts to reinterpret those laws in light of the new data and new attitudes with the exception of a very recent decision by a federal district court in California, which has been appealed.[3]

Indeed, there now seems little hope for a change through legislative channels, at least in the near future. In March 1981, the Select Commission on Immigration and Refugee Policy, which had been appointed by Congress three years earlier to review the nation's immigration laws, issued a final report that failed to recommend any alteration in the policy of excluding homosexuals, although it did put forward other proposals for reform. Members of the commission reportedly felt that such a recommendation would be so controversial that it would have a detrimental affect on the group's other suggestions.[4]

Did the court define a "homosexual"?

No. Nor is there any clear definition of the terms *psychopathic personality*, and *sexual deviation*. A very important problem here is the imprecision with which such terms are used, and the frequency with which people are unthinkingly treated in the same way. Some guidance as to what the court intended in *Boutilier* may, however, be obtained from the facts presented in that case. The alien in *Boutilier* had engaged regularly in homosexual conduct over a period of several years, both before, and after, his last entry into the United States. He had also engaged on "three or four occasions," in heterosexual conduct. The court described the alien's activities as involving a "continued course" of homosexual conduct. Although the courts might not regard isolated and unrepeated homosexual conduct as proof of a "psychopathic personality" or "sexual deviation," it should be assumed that any pattern of homosexual activity continuing up to the time of attempted entry into the United States, may permit the exclusion of an alien.

These rules may seem vague and imprecise—and they are. The alien in *Boutilier* argued that it was unfair to punish him by deportation, when he had not been given a fair warning of the applicable rules when he entered the United States. The claim was, however, rejected by the court. On the other hand, a lower federal court held on an earlier occasion, that these rules were impermissibly vague.[5] Perhaps the Supreme Court will one day agree.

How does the Immigration and Naturalization Service (INS) apply the provisions under which gay aliens may be excluded from the United States?

The INS position is that until the law providing for the exclusion of gay aliens is changed by Congress, the agency must enforce it by barring the entry, into the United States, of persons known to be homosexual, or by commencing deportation proceedings against such aliens already in the country.

In 1980, however, the INS did promulgate new guidelines for the *enforcement* of the immigration laws at the nation's borders; these are more favorable to gays than the agency's previous practices. Under the new guidelines, only persons who make an "unsolicited, unambiguous oral or written admission of homosexuality" to immigration inspectors will be subject to exclusion. Wearing buttons or T-shirts or possessing literature supporting gay rights, will not by themselves be grounds for further questioning.

If, however, one wears a button or other emblem that states "I Am Gay," or if one is identified to the immigration inspectors by a traveling companion as being gay, that alien may be questioned in private. If the alien answers no, he or she may not be detained for further examination. If the alien answers yes, he or she will be asked to sign a statement to that effect, and, whether or not the statement is signed, will be referred to an immigration judge for an exclusion proceeding. No search may be performed for the purpose of seeking evidence of homosexuality. The new guidelines are still being followed, but how long they will continue in effect is unclear.

What about aliens who have already entered the United States?

In most situations, immigration officers are unaware of an alien's sexual preferences at the time of entry. The question of excludability frequently arises after the alien has entered the United States, usually in the context of a deportation proceeding. Under Section 241 of the Immigration and Nationality Act, an alien is subject to deportation from the United States on a variety of grounds. The rules are complex, but there is no doubt that homosexual conduct may, in some situations, permit deportation.

The first ground for deportation under Section 241, includes situations in which an alien was excludable at the time of his last entry into the United States. The idea here is that an alien who could have been excluded should not be permitted to remain here merely because that fact escaped notice at the time of entry. The effect of this provision is to make all aliens who were excludable at the time of their last entry on the basis of a "psychopathic personality" or "sexual deviation," permanently subject to deportation. In *Boutilier*, for example, the alien first entered the United States in 1955, and reentered in 1959. He applied for citizenship in 1963, and ultimately acknowledged, in the course of the naturalization process that he had from time to time prior to 1959 engaged in homosexual conduct. The Supreme Court held in 1967, twelve years after his first entry, and eight years after his latest entry, that he was deportable because he had been excludable in 1959.

The critical date for determining excludability, and hence for deportability under the first ground, is the alien's last entry. This does not necessarily mean, however, that conduct that occurs within the United States may not be relevant. It is possible that evidence of postentry homosexual conduct may be used in combination with evidence of preentry conduct to establish the existence of a "psychopathic personality" or "sexual deviation" at the time of entry. More important, homosexual conduct within the United States may permit exclusion or deportation of an alien if, after the conduct has occurred, he leaves the United States and then returns. The Supreme Court's decision in *Boutilier* illustrates the dangers of such departures and reentries. The alien in that case left and later reentered the United States in 1959, and by so doing, made his homosexual conduct within the United States between 1955 and 1959 grounds for his deportation.

Does this mean that I should never leave the United States, even temporarily?

It is not quite that simple. The Supreme Court held in 1963, in *Rosenberg* v. *Fleuti*,[7] that an "entry" after only a very brief departure from the United States—in that case, an afternoon's visit to Mexico—will not always be counted for this purpose. The rules here are not exact, but it may be assumed that courts will take into account the duration of the absence from the United States, the purpose of the visit, what travel documents and other formalities were involved, and any other facts pertinent to measure the significance of the departure. Uncertainty is increased by the fact that the court was divided in *Rosenberg*, and it is by no means clear that it would reach the same conclusion today. The best advice here is caution. It is wise to assume that any departure, however brief, involves a measure of possible danger. Unnecessary departures should be avoided. When you balance the relative advantages of a week in Florida and a week in Nassau, take full account of the added risks of a new entry into the United States.

What if I am convicted of a criminal offense based on homosexual conduct?

An important ground for deportation under Section 241 is conviction of certain criminal offenses. Two alternative formulas will permit deportation. An alien may be deported if he or she is convicted of a crime "involving moral turpitude," within five years after entry into the United States, and is either sentenced to confinement, or confined in a prison or corrective institution for a year or more. A sentence even if it is not served, will suffice. Although the conviction must occur within five years after entry, each new entry into the United States will have the effect of extending the application of the statute. The requirement of a sentence to confinement may raise important technical questions. One federal court has held that a person convicted of "open lewdness" and given a suspended sentence under the New Jersey Sex Offenders Act was not sentenced to confinement within the meaning of the deportation laws.[8] The court emphasized that the New Jersey act had humanitarian, not punitive, goals and that the sentence was only a technical means of assuring treatment for the convicted person.

Alternatively, deportation may be ordered even without a prison sentence if an alien is convicted of two crimes "involving moral turpitude," provided that they do not arise out of a "single scheme" of criminal misconduct. It is important that no time limitation has been placed on this rule. Two such convictions will permit deportation, no matter how long they occur after entry.

The central question under both formulas obviously is whether a crime involves "moral turpitude." Although considerable attention has been given to that question by the courts and by the Immigration Service, no clear rules have been developed. It is said that the governing issue is the "inherent nature" of the crime, as defined by statute or interpreted by the courts. Some examples may help to clarify the confusing positions that have been adopted on this matter. It has been held that indecent exposure, without evidence of motive or circumstances, does not involve "moral turpitude"; that solicitation in a public restroom does involve "moral turpitude"; that consensual sodomy does involve "moral turpitude"; and that an undefined offense of "gross indecency" under Canadian law does involve "moral turpitude."[9] These and other similar results give us little meaningful guidance regarding the nature of the offenses that involve "moral turpitude," but it is wise to assume that any criminal conviction based on homosexual conduct may satisfy the requirements of Section 241.

The severity of the deportation requirement makes it clear that any alien who is charged with a criminal offense should obtain careful advice before responding to the charge. Be certain to emphasize to your attorney that you are an alien and subject to the dangers of deportation under Section 241. Aliens have sometimes bargained with prosecuting attorneys and pleaded guilty to a lesser offense, only to find that they have become subject to deportation.[10]

I entered the United States on a nonimmigrant visa and now wish to have my status adjusted so that I can remain in the United States permanently. Are there any dangers involved if I make such a request?

Yes. An application to adjust status permits a new examination to determine if an alien should be expelled from the United States.[11] Let us assume, for example, that an alien has lawfully entered the United States as a student, and that his sexual conduct at the time of his entry was such that he could not have been excluded on the ground of a "psychopathic personality," or "sexual deviation." If the alien has, since his entry into the United States, engaged in conduct that would support a finding that he has now developed a "psychopathic personality" or "sexual deviation," an adjustment of status creates new risks of expulsion from the United States. It may well be, of course, that the terms of an alien's entry will require his or her departure from the United States unless an

adjustment of status is obtained, thus leaving little realistic
alternative. No effort to obtain an adjustment should, however, be undertaken unnecessarily, or without careful consideration of the possible dangers.

I wish to become a naturalized American citizen. Will homosexual conduct disqualify me?

It may, although there have been some recent judicial
opinions on this issue that are encouraging.

The immigration laws provide that, in addition to various
requirements regarding residence in the United States, a
petitioner for naturalization must be, and have been, for the
previous five years, "a person of good moral character, attached to the principles of the Constitution of the United
States, and well disposed to the good order and happiness of
the United States."[12] For purposes of determining "moral
character," the courts take into account a petitioner's "conduct and acts at any time prior" to the statutory five-year
period.[13]

The term *good moral character* is never fully defined.
However, the immigration laws indicate that a person lacks
"good moral character" if he or she has in the past given false
testimony for the purpose of obtaining immigration or naturalization benefits, or if he or she has been confined to a
penal institution during the previous five years for an aggre-
gate period of one hundred eighty days or more.[14] These
automatic exclusions may result in the disqualification of some
gay applicants for naturalization.

And for others, the road may still be treacherous. It is well
settled that the burden of proving "good moral character" is
on the petitioner,[15] and any doubts may be resolved against
the petitioner.[16] A lower New York State court took the
position in 1968, in *Matter of Schmidt,* that if one admits that
she committed homosexual acts during the five years prior to
the filing of a petition for naturalization, she should be denied
naturalization for want of "good moral character."[17] The court
acknowledged that the petitioner in that case had not violated
any criminal statute, and that all of her activities had been in
private between consenting adults, but averred that the "ordinary man or woman" would find the petitioner's habits
inconsistent with "good moral character."

In contrast, a federal district court in New York in 1971,

held in *In re Labady*, that a petitioner's private homosexual conduct did not prevent his naturalization.[18] The court emphasized that a judge's individual beliefs or preferences should not be controlling, and that the standard should instead be "the ethical standards current at the time." It then ruled that private conduct may not be the basis for the denial of naturalization. The court noted that in recent years there has been a gradual relaxation of the severe penalties heretofore imposed on homosexual conduct, and a slow change in public attitudes as well. And it observed that adultery and private heterosexual conduct between unmarried adults has not prevented naturalization in other cases.

Similarly, in *In re Brodie* in 1975, a federal court in Oregon granted a petition for naturalization; private homosexual conduct was not considered inconsistent with "good moral character."[19] The court ruled, among other things, that the standards for exclusion were not identical to those for naturalization. Indeed, the court admitted that the petitioner, Brodie, could have been kept out of the country at the time of his original entry into the United States, but decided that that fact by itself would not necessarily prevent his naturalization.

Even more recently, in *Nemetz* v. *Immigration and Naturalization Service*, a federal appeals court in 1981 ordered the INS to grant the naturalization petition of a forty-one-year-old gay male, even though he admitted that he was a "practicing homosexual," and lived in a state (Virginia) that still made it a crime to engage in consensual sodomy. The INS had attempted to deny his petition on the basis of his residence in Virginia, and the federal district court had upheld the denial. The appeals court rejected this view entirely. "[W]hether a person is of good moral character for purposes of naturalization is a question of federal law," said the court, and cannot be left to an "accident of geography" such as the fact that the petitioner lived in Virginia rather than Illinois, where consensual sodomy is not a crime. The court concluded: "Nemetz's homosexual activity cannot serve as the basis for a denial of a finding of good moral character because it has been purely private, consensual and without harm to the public."[20]

Labady, Brodie, and *Nemetz*, taken together, offer new hope to permanent residents who wish to obtain U.S. citizenship, who, because of their homosexuality, faced problems in the past.

Aren't inquiries by the government into sexual habits and preferences invasions of privacy, and therefore unconstitutional?

Under most circumstances, they would be. However, the courts have generally treated the immigration laws as a world apart, an area of the law in which the Bill of Rights simply does not apply, or applies in a sharply diluted form.[21]

What should I do if I am interrogated by an immigration official?

Immediately ask to consult an attorney or other competent adviser before you answer any questions. You must avoid making damaging admissions, but you should also remember not to give the impression that you might refuse to give information to which the service is entitled under the law.

Should I lie?

No. Lying exposes you to the possibility of additional penalties, including the loss of whatever status you hope to be granted.[22] As already stated, according to the immigration laws, lying in order to obtain immigration or naturalization benefits, is inconsistent with "good moral character." Moreover, deportation is permitted when a visa has been procured by fraud, or by willful misrepresentation of a material fact.[23]

What should I do if I am uncertain as to how these rules apply to me, or if I am considering a change in my status?

You should consult an attorney. This book is designed to give you general guidance and information, not to act as a substitute for expert advice regarding any specific situation. If you have any doubts as to your situation, or are considering any step that might trigger an important change in that situation, it would be wise to obtain such advice. If you are uncertain as to whom to consult, contact local gay-activist groups, the nearest ACLU chapter, or your local legal-assistance office. If they cannot offer help, ask them to refer you to an appropriate attorney. You should remember that you are a member of two groups that have long been treated by the courts and others with special harshness: aliens, and those who have engaged in homosexual conduct. Various administrative and judicial remedies may be available to you, but the proper course to follow in each case should be carefully discussed with a qualified adviser, after all of the possible dangers have been thoroughly explored and evaluated.[24]

NOTES

1. 8 U.S.C. §1182(a).
2. 387 U.S. 118 (1967).
3. See Lesbian/Gay Freedom Day Committee v. U.S. Immigration & Naturalization Service, 541 F. Supp. 569 (N.D. Ca. 1982). In that decision, involving two different cases, the court overturned an order excluding a British subject who had made an unsolicited statement to an immigration inspector that he was gay, on the ground that the Public Health Service had failed to issue a medical certificate stating that the alien was afflicted with "sexual deviation" or a "mental defect," which is a requirement under the Immigration and Nationality Act. (Since 1979, the Public Health Service has refused as a matter of policy to issue such certificates merely on the basis of homosexuality, the Surgeon General having determined the homosexuality per se is not a mental disease or defect.) In the companion case, the court ruled that the Immigration and Naturalization Service could no longer pursue its policy of excluding aliens on the basis of homosexuality alone, for two different reasons. First, to do so when homosexuality is no longer considered a mental disorder or medical illness violates the intent of Congress that such exclusions be based on valid medical reasons. (The district court specifically concluded that *Boutilier* was inapplicable. The court stated: *"Boutilier* does not preclude the Court from finding that Congress did not intend that homosexuals be excluded from entry into the United States solely because they are homosexuals once medical authorities have determined that homosexuality is not a medical illness, mental disorder, or sexual deviation, and the Court finds this to be the congressional intent.") Secondly, the Court held that the policy of excluding homosexuals per se violates the First Amendment rights of American citizens to hear the views of and associate with homosexuals from abroad, at least where there is a desire to share information about homosexuals and homosexuality in both the United States and other countries.

   The Immigration and Naturalization Service has appealed the district court's decision in both cases.
4. See *New York Times,* Feb. 15, 1981, 28.
5. Fleuti v. Rosenberg, 302 F.2d 652 (9th Cir. 1962), *vacated and remanded on other grounds,* 374 U.S. 449 (1963).

6. 8 U.S.C. §1251.

7. 374 U.S. 449 (1963).

8. Holzapfel v. Wyrsch, 259 F.2d 890 (3d Cir. 1958).

9. See Velez-Lozano v. Immigration & Naturalization Service, 463 F.2d 1305 (D.C. Cir. 1972); Hudson v. Esperdy, 290 F.2d 879 (2d Cir. 1961); Marinelli v. Ryan, 285 F.2d 474 (2d Cir. 1961).

10. See, e.g. Velez-Lozano v. Immigration & Naturalization Service, *supra* note 9. The Immigration and Nationality Act also provides that a person convicted of a crime and otherwise deportable may escape deportation if he or she receives a "full and unconditional pardon," or if the sentencing court recommends to the Attorney General, either when it imposes its sentence or within thirty days afterwards, that the alien not be deported. 8 U.S.C. §1251 (b).

11. Campos v. United States Immigration & Naturalization Service, 402 F.2d 758 (9th Cir. 1968).

12. 8 U.S.C. §1427(a) (3).

13. 8 U.S.C. §1427(e).

14. 8 U.S.C. §1101(f).

15. Berenyi v. District Director, 385 U.S. 630 (1967).

16. United States v. MacIntosh, 283 U.S. 605 (1931).

17. Matter of Schmidt, 56 Misc. 2d 456, 289 N.Y.S. 2d 89 (Sup. Ct. 1968).

18. In re Labady, 326 F. Supp. 924 (S.D. N.Y. 1971).

19. In re Brodie, 394 F. Supp. 1208 (D. Ore. 1975).

20. In re Nemetz, 647 F.2d 432 (4th Cir. 1981).

21. See, e.g. Kleindienst v. Mandel, 408 U.S. 753 (1972).

22. See, e.g. Kovacs v. United States, 476 F.2d 843 (2d Cir. 1973).

23. See, e.g. Granduxe y Marino v. Murff, 183 F. Supp. 565 (S.D. N.Y. 1959), *aff'd per curiam*, 378 F.2d 330 (2d Cir.), *cert. denied*, 364 U.S. 824 (1960).

24. The authors gratefully acknowledge the assistance and advice of Arthur C. Helton, Esq., of The Lawyers Committee for International Human Rights, in the preparation of this chapter.

VII

Housing and Public Accommodations

Housing

Gay people are now afforded little protection against discrimination in housing, except in California and Wisconsin and in a few municipalities elsewhere where there are gay rights ordinances. They may be denied the rental of an apartment or the purchase of a house precisely because of their homosexuality, or for no stated reason whatsoever. However, gay people are not totally without rights when they deal with landlords, homeowners, and real estate agents, even in those parts of the country without protective legislation. The purpose of this chapter is to help you to understand the general extent of those rights as they now exist, in anticipation of the day when discrimination in housing on the basis of one's sexual orientation, will be totally outlawed.

To what extent do federal laws prohibit discrimination in housing?

Since the Civil War, Congress has passed many laws that relate to discrimination in housing. The Civil Rights Act of 1866,[1] the first such statute enacted, assures equal property rights to nonwhites, as well as whites, and it has been held to apply to individual sellers, as well as to the government.[2] The Civil Rights Act of 1870[3] contains a general guarantee of equal rights for nonwhites, including the right "to make and enforce contracts." Title VI of the Civil Rights Act of 1964[4] prohibits discrimination under any program or activity receiving federal financial assistance on the basis of race, color, or national origin. And Title VIII of the Civil Rights Act of 1968,[5] the most important and comprehensive of these statutes, bars all discrimination in the sale or rental of housing on the basis of race, color, religion, natural origin, or sex.[6]

Congress has had before it since 1975, a bill that would extend equal rights in housing to gay people as well, but has failed so far to act, and the chance of passage in the near future seems slim.[7]

What about state laws?

Most states have a statute similar to Title VIII of the Civil Rights Act of 1968, but only one—Wisconsin—has seen fit to include "sexual orientation" in the list of prohibited categories of discrimination. Another state, California, has a statute (the Unruh Civil Rights Act) that has been construed by the courts to prohibit all forms of arbitrary discrimination by landlords, including discrimination against gay people. (It is unclear whether that principle also extends to private homeowners who try to sell their houses.)[8]

Several municipalities have enacted antidiscrimination ordinances, including San Francisco; Los Angeles; Philadelphia; Washington, D.C.; Minneapolis; Madison, Wisconsin; Columbus, Ohio; and Ann Arbor, Michigan.

A curious footnote: in January of 1982, the voters of Austin, Texas, were asked to approve a *pro*discrimination ordinance that would have permitted landlords the "moral discretion" to refuse housing to anyone on the basis of sexual orientation (a right landlords probably already had under the law anyway). The proposal was defeated by a ratio of 2 to 1.[9]

What protection does a gay person have against discrimination by a landlord, or by a broker or homeowner, in places without gay rights legislation?

In general, there is nothing to prohibit discrimination because someone is gay. For example, the law has traditionally afforded landlords enormous discretion in making renting decisions; in most jurisdictions, they may rent to whomever they choose, so long as they do not discriminate in a way that has been specifically outlawed by the legislature. In a recent notorious decision in New York, a landlord was upheld in his refusal to rent an apartment to a black, divorced woman despite a law prohibiting discrimination on the basis of race, marital status, or sex, because he was able to convince the court that his real reason for discrimination was the fact that the applicant was a lawyer, and therefore someone likely to know—and to assert—her legal rights. (Lawyers, under New York law, are not a protected class.) A landlord can, said the court, "decide not to rent to singles because they are too noisy, or not to rent to bald-headed men because he has been told they give wild parties. He can bar his premises to the lowest strata of society, should he choose, or to the highest, if that be his personal desire."[10]

Yet a gay person who is denied a house or an apartment may have a claim against the landlord on a ground other than discrimination against the buyer's sexual orientation. Some states and localities, for instance, have laws that prohibit discrimination on the basis of marital status.[11] In a recent case in Washington State, which has such a law, a landlord was held to have acted illegally because she had told two males who were looking for an apartment together that the apartment would be rented only to married couples.[12]

If you do not know the extent of the protection offered by the law where you live, you should find out if your city or state government has a human rights commission, and make inquiries there—or at the local tenants' rights organization, if there is one.

Does that mean that a landlord may evict a gay tenant just because he or she is gay?

Not necessarily. If the tenant is protected by a written lease, the landlord usually cannot evict him or her without proof that a specific provision of the lease has been violated. Unfortunately, many leases are blatantly one-sided and contain clauses with strict regulations as to how a tenant may use an apartment, and who may occupy it with him. Some leases, for instance, limit occupancy to the person who signed the lease, or to someone related to him or her "by blood or marriage." If your lease contained such a clause, and your lover moved into your apartment with you, your landlord might seek to evict both of you, and he would probably succeed (although in some jurisdictions you might be able to claim that this amounted to discrimination on the basis of marital status).

In some places, tenants are protected by special rent-control or rent-stabilization laws that limit not only the amount of rent that a landlord may charge, but the circumstances under which a landlord may evict a tenant. Every tenant should make himself aware of the existence and scope of any laws of this kind.

No matter what the particular circumstances, and no matter what the applicable law, a tenant may be evicted only pursuant to a court order issued as the result of a formal eviction proceeding. The tenant is always entitled to prior notice of such a proceeding. If your landlord threatens to evict you, or serves notice of an eviction proceeding, see a lawyer immediately.

What is the law governing condominiums and cooperatives?

The past two decades have seen an explosion in the popularity of nontraditional forms of housing—notably condominium and cooperative apartments.

Both involve ownership interests held in common with neighbors. A condominium is a dwelling unit (it can be a townhouse, a high-rise apartment, or virtually any other kind of living space) that one owns along with an interest in facilities maintained by all the property owners in the same building or project. A board or members' association manages those common areas and makes rules governing life in the building. Although it too is usually run by a board, a cooperative apartment is quite different, at least in theory. The occupant of a co-op does not actually own his apartment; rather, along with the other tenants in the building, he holds stock in the corporation that owns and operates it, and that stock entitles him to a "proprietary lease" to his particular apartment. Co-ops are most common in the Northeast and in parts of Florida.

The law generally allows condominium or co-op owners, at least as much discretion in selecting a buyer, as it does an ordinary homeowner. Thus, in most instances, there is little a gay person can do to challenge a condominium or co-op owner's refusal to sell to him, unless of course there is a statute specifically outlawing such discrimination.

Co-ops present particularly difficult problems for gays. Since they are owned (in theory) by all the occupants of a building, they are subject to special restrictions. Typically, a prospective buyer must meet the approval of the board of directors of the corporation, as well as the tenant-owner. These restrictions generally apply to other kinds of transfers as well. Thus, a gay person may not simply give his co-op to a lover or friend as a married person may to his spouse or child, even under the provisions of a will, and even when the other person actually resides with the tenant-owner. He or she must first seek the permission of the board. In the case of a will, the tenant-owner who wants to leave a co-op to his or her lover, should take steps either to make that person a co-owner immediately, or to obtain the board's prospective approval.

May a gay person be denied a mortgage on the basis of sexual orientation?

Generally yes. The personal life of an applicant for a mortgage should be irrelevant to the determination of whether the applicant is credit-worthy. In the past many banks and savings and loan associations (like many employers) have viewed gay people as inherently unstable because of their unorthodox life-styles. As a result, gays have been denied mortgages on the ground that they were too much of a financial risk.

There is little federal or state law to prohibit such discrimination against gay people per se. However, federal law and many state laws, now prohibit discrimination in credit on the basis of sex or marital status; these categories may be of use in certain cases when banks deny mortgages.[13]

May gays be excluded from participation in public-housing programs?

Gay people are often not eligible for participation in public-housing programs, not because these programs specifically exclude gays, but because preference is usually given to traditional household units. For example, federal-housing programs for the poor were originally limited to "families," and the term *family* was limited to two or more people related by blood, marriage, or adoption. The definition of *family* has since been expanded to cover various categories of single people, and now includes virtually all singles, but nontraditional households are still placed last on the eligibility list for federal-housing programs, except for the elderly or handicapped.[14] Moveover, the participation of single people who are neither old nor disabled in federal low-income programs, is specifically limited by law to a maximum of fifteen percent of the units under the jurisdiction of any public-housing agency.[15]

The courts have yet to determine whether all such schemes violate the Constitution, but at least one important case suggests that the most blatantly discriminatory schemes do. In 1973, in *United States Department of Agriculture* v. *Moreno*,[16] the Supreme Court considered the rules used to determine eligibility for participation in the federal food stamp program. Eligibility was based on households, rather than individuals, and the term *household* included only groups whose members were all related to each other (as well as single people living alone). The legislative history of the statute indicated that Congress had defined *household* in this way to exclude "hippies" and "hippie communes" from the food-stamp program. The court declared the restriction "clearly irrelevant to the stated purposes of the Act," which were "to safeguard the health and well-being of the Nation's population and raise levels of nutrition among low-level households," and struck it down. In so doing, the court declared, "[I]f the constitutional conception of 'equal protection of the laws' means anything, it must at the very least mean that a bare congressional desire to harm a politically unpopular group cannot constitute a *legitimate* governmental interest."[17]

A more recent Supreme Court case, *Boraas* v. *Belle Terre*,[18] indicates that, nevertheless, the government has the right to promote traditional family life, at least if it does so in a way that is not overly broad or harsh. In this case, the court upheld an ordinance in a suburban community outside New York City that prohibited more than two unrelated people from living together in the same household. Justice Douglas, in writing the opinion, intoned, "The police power is not confined to elimination of filth, stench, and unhealthy places. It is ample to lay out zones where family values, youth values, and the blessings of quiet seclusion and clean air make the area a sanctuary for people."[19]

A more recent case makes it clear that *Boraas* has its limits; for example, the government may not limit households only to members of the immediate family.[20] Yet *Boraas* is still troubling for its suggestion that the government may enact laws that punish or prohibit altogether households that deviate from the traditional mode.

What is the best guidance for gays on housing rights?

1. *Learn about housing rights in general*. All tenants have certain statutory and judicial rights, especially under rent-control laws, building codes, and local ordinances. There are also judicially created doctrines that protect tenants in certain situations, including certain warranties. The following two books are useful resources: Blumberg and Grow, *The Rights of Tenants* (1978; (one of the books in the ACLU series on individual rights); and Striker and Shapiro, *Super Tenant* (1978, rev. ed.); (subtitled *New York City Tenant Handbook*, but helpful for residents of other localities as well). Tenants' councils and organizations are also good sources for information in many areas.

2. *Use tenant organizations*. Such organizations are not only sources of information, but they can also be used to produce legislative change and to protect individual rights.

3. *Get a lease, read it carefully, and have each member of the household sign it*.

4. *Where applicable, challenge discriminatory conduct on the basis of a traditionally protected class such as race, creed, color, national origin, or sex*. If such discrimination exists, contact your local attorney general, the state or local housing administrator, the local human rights commission, or the Department of Housing and Urban Development's Office of Fair Housing and Equal Opportunity.

5. *Where there is a state or local fair-housing ordinance that specifically prohibits discrimination on the basis of sexual preference, contact the local authority indicated in the ordinance*.

6. *Seek legal representation*, particularly if you are threatened with eviction. Go to legal aid or community legal services if you qualify. You may also contact gay organizations—which are listed in the Appendix—for legal referrals. For major cases of discrimination, contact the local ACLU chapter. The addresses are also listed in the Appendix.

7. *Legislation*. Work for local, state, and national fair-housing laws that prohibit discrimination on the basis of sexual orientation.

8. *Have a will*. Since under present laws, marriages between gays are not recognized as legally valid, it is especially important to execute a will to provide for the disposition of property upon death. Otherwise, the state law of intestate succession will determine who will receive the property in the estate. Those whom you wish to benefit may be excluded, even if they shared in the purchase of property and, implicitly or explicitly, you have agreed that if one of you should die, the other will own all the property. (See chapter VIII, "The Gay Family," for a more detailed discussion of property rights.)

Public Accommodations

Another area in which gays sometimes suffer discriminatory treatment is public accommodations, which includes bars, restaurants, discotheques, hotels, and motels. Sometimes the discrimination is embodied in the law itself. Until 1971, for example, regulations of the New York City Department of Consumer Affairs prohibited homosexuals from congregating in cabarets and dancing clubs, and prohibited the employment of homosexuals in cabarets in any capacity. Any such laws or regulations still on the books now would undoubtedly be subject to constitutional attack. That such prohibitions could exist, however, is indicative of an attitude toward gay people that has only recently begun to change.

Has Congress passed any laws prohibiting discrimination against gays in public accommodations?
Not yet. Presently, as with housing, federal legislation extends only to such categories as race, color, religion, national origin, and sex. Legislation has been introduced in Congress, however, which would amend the civil rights laws to prohibit discrimination in public accommodations based on "affectional or sexual orientation."

Do any states have legislation that would prohibit discrimination against gays in public accommodations?
One state, Wisconsin, has adopted legislation protecting gays against such discrimination, and similar bills have been introduced in many other states as well. California has a

statute—the Unruh Civil Rights Act—that has been interpreted by the courts of that state to bar all forms of arbitrary
discrimination by business establishments, including discrimination against gay people.[21]

**Do any cities or municipalities in the United States have
local laws prohibiting discrimination in public accommodations based on sexual orientation?**

Yes. Local laws have been adopted in many municipalities
prohibiting discrimination in public accommodations based
on sexual orientation, including Ann Arbor, Michigan; Austin,
Texas; Berkeley; Champaign, Illinois; Los Angeles; Madison,
Wisconsin; Minneapolis; Philadelphia; San Francisco; Tuscon,
Arizona; and Washington, D.C.

**What should gays do in an instance of discrimination in
one of the cities with a local ordinance prohibiting such
discrimination?**

Most of these ordinances are administered by a city commission or department of human rights, and procedures are
established for filing complaints with these agencies. It is
advisable to secure the assistance of a lawyer in filing a
complaint. If you do not have a lawyer, you should contact a
local gay organization or the local ACLU affiliate.

**Is there any protection against discrimination based on
sexual orientation in places that do not have laws specifically
prohibiting it?**

Only if the discrimination can be brought within the scope
of some other legally proscribed discrimination. (For example, both local and state laws in some places make discrimination based on sex or marital status illegal.)

If the public accommodations are government operated, as
are many parks, beaches, swimming pools, and campgrounds,
you might have a claim under the constitutional guarantee of
equal protection of the laws, which in general requires the
government to act evenhandedly unless it has a reasonable
basis for not doing so. To date, however, there have been no
reported cases on such a challenge.

Is it legal for gays to dance together in public places?

It is not illegal, per se, but gays in some localities can still expect to be harassed and possibly arrested on charges of disorderly conduct or a similar offense for dancing together in nongay establishments. These charges should be contested on the grounds that the conduct is not disorderly or a violation of any law. New York's highest court has held that indulgence in the inference that men in a grill were "from their dress and makeup, homosexuals does not support the additional inference that they would create disorder." In another case, the court said, "It is reasonable to think that even though he dresses strangely a homosexual may be orderly."[22] The court then said, "there is no sound reason to distinguish between the actions of homosexuals and that of heterosexuals with respect to the dancing of slow dances."[23] Where there are local or state ordinances prohibiting discrimination against gays in public accommodations, there is a legal remedy for any such discrimination. In one of the few cases that have arisen under such ordinances, an Austin, Texas, bar was convicted of violating that city's antidiscrimination laws by prohibiting same-sex dancing.[24]

NOTES

1. 42 U.S.C. §1982.
2. Jones v. Alfred H. Mayer Co., 392 U.S. 409 (1968) (an individual could not discriminate against a black who wanted to buy property).
3. 42 U.S.C. §1981.
4. 42 U.S.C. §2000d, *et seq*.
5. 42 U.S.C. §3601, *et seq*.
6. 42 U.S.C. §3604.
7. During the Ninety-sixth Congress, this bill carried the number S.2081 (Tsongas, Weicker, and Moynihan) in the Senate, and H.R.2074 (Waxman and Weiss) in the House of Representatives.
8. WISC. STAT. ANN. §101.22; Hubert v. Williams, 184 Cal. Rptr. 161 (Super Ct. 1982). See generally *Equal Employment in Housing* (Prentice–Hall), which is a looseleaf service that contains all the various state fair-housing and human rights laws pertaining to housing.
9. See *New York Times*, Jan. 18, 1982, A17.
10. Kramarsky v. Stahl Management, 92 Misc. 2d 1030, 401 N.Y.S. 2d 943 (Sup. Ct. N.Y. Co. 1977).
11. See, e.g. COLO. REV. STAT. ANN. §69–7–5; NEW YORK STATE EXECUTIVE LAW §296; ORE. REV. STAT. §659.033.
12. Loveland v. Leslie, 21 Wash. App. 84, 583 P.2d 664 (Ct. App. 1978). For another case on marital status discrimination, see Hudson

View Properties v. Weiss, 106 Misc. 2d 251, 431 N.Y.S. 2d 632 (N.Y.C. Civil Ct. 1980), *rev'd,* 109 Misc. 2d 589, 442 N.Y.S. 2d 367 (App. Term 1981), *rev'd,* 86 App. Div. 2d 803, 448 N.Y.S. 2d 649 (1st Dept. 1982). Hudson View Properties v. Weiss involved an unmarried heterosexual couple, but the court noted, "A prohibition against discrimination based on marital status is consistent with both evolving notions of morality and the realities of contemporary urban society, when couples openly live in heterosexual and homosexual units without sanction of state or clergy." But see Avest Seventh Corp. v. Ringelheim, 109 Misc.2d 284, 440 N.Y.S. 2d 159 (N.Y.C. Civil Ct. 1981).

13. See Equal Credit Opportunity Act of 1975, 15 U.S.C. §1961, *et seq.*

14. 42 U.S.C. §1437a(3). See generally *The Housing Needs of "Non-Traditional" Households,* published by the Office of Policy Development and Research of the U.S. Department of Housing and Urban Development (1979).

15. 42 U.S.C. §1437a(3).

16. 413 U.S. 528 (1973).

17. *Id.* at 534.

18. 416 U.S. 1 (1974).

19. *Id.* at 9.

20. Moore v. East Cleveland, 431 U.S. 494 (1977).

21. WISC. STAT. ANN. §942.04; Marina Point, Ltd. v. Wolfson, 30 Cal. 3d 721, 180 Cal Rpts. 496, 640p.2d 115 (1982).

22. Kerma Restaurant Corp. v. State Liquor Authority, 21 N.Y. 2d 111, 115, 286 N.Y.S. 2d 822, 824–25 (1967).

23. Becker v. New York State Liquor Authority, 21 N.Y. 2d 289, 291, 287 N.Y.S. 2d 400, 401 (1967).

24. Texas v. Driskill Bar and Grill, reported in Oct. 1979 *Gay Rights Advocates Newsletter* (San Francisco).

VIII

The Gay Family

Many gay people now live together as "families," and seek to obtain the benefits that society and the government confer on married couples. There is no reason in principle why two gays should be prevented from entering into a relationship that is deemed, for all purposes, to be a lawful "marriage." Nonetheless, the law has consistently refused to recognize gay marriages.

The law now clearly discriminates in favor of heterosexual marital relationships. An elaborate body of laws has developed with respect to the benefits, rights, and privileges of persons who commit themselves to such relationships. Marital partners have certain advantages in paying their income, gift, and estate taxes. They may inherit from one another without a will; they may own property in tenancy by the entirety; they may run businesses at lower cost in taxes; each may recover for the wrongful death of the other; they may adopt children more easily than singles; and they may lawfully have sexual relations. Most of these and other benefits are denied to those who elect not to marry, or who are not permitted to marry. Private organizations such as airlines, insurance companies, and banks, also offer their goods and services on terms that discriminate in favor of married persons.

This chapter describes the legal barriers to gay marriages, and the financial disabilities that result for gays because they cannot lawfully marry. It explores alternative means of obtaining the financial benefits that are based on marriage. Finally, it discusses the problems of gays who have natural children of their own, or who seek to adopt or care for children.

Gay Marriages

Does every state have a law forbidding marriage licenses for same-sex marriages?
No. Every state has marriage laws that define what requirements must be met before two people may obtain a marriage license. Such requirements usually specify that the applicants must be of a certain age, not closely related by blood, single, and free from certain types of venereal disease. There is apparently only one state that specifically requires that applicants be members of the opposite sex.[1] There are, however, in the language of the marriage laws of a number of states, references to "husband and wife," or "man and woman."

Are gay marriages now recognized by any state?
No.

What are the consequences of the states' refusal to recognize gay marriages?
When a state refuses to recognize a marriage, the couple may not gain legal benefits that are conditional upon marriage. Those benefits are described more fully below. It also means that neither partner is entitled, as a matter of law, to the financial support of the other (which, if married, both might be entitled to, depending on the jurisdiction).

What are the risks of obtaining a marriage license from the state without the state being aware that you intend to enter a same-sex marriage?
You may be accused of fraud, although there are no reported cases.

What is the significance of a religious ceremony purporting to join together two people of the same sex?
Since no state has yet recognized as valid a marriage between members of the same sex, such ceremonies have no

legal significance. In fact, they are usually not described as "marriage ceremonies," but as ceremonies of "holy union." Whatever their significance to the participants, "holy unions" do not entitle anyone to the legal benefits of marriage.

Is it unlawful to perform or to participate in such a ceremony?

No.

Is the fact that the states do not recognize such religious ceremonies a violation of freedom of religion?

Probably not. The United States Supreme Court has held that a state may outlaw polygamous marriages as contrary to public policy.[2] It is unclear to what extent the principle underlying this case extends to other religious rites that may offend large segments of the American population.

No couple has yet sought to obtain legal recognition of a "holy union" under the doctrine of religious liberty, but it seems unlikely that such a challenge would succeed, given the present legal climate.

Have the courts ever upheld the rights of gays to obtain marriage licenses?

No. Gays in Minnesota,[3] Kentucky,[4] and Washington,[5] have unsuccessfully challenged the denial of marriage licenses in state courts. In each case the court held that the couple did not have a right to obtain a license because the drafters of the applicable legislation contemplated heterosexual marriages only. The United States Supreme Court has not yet explicitly ruled on this question.

Although no gay couple has attempted to obtain legal recognition in this country of a foreign marriage, it is unlikely that such an effort would be successful.[6]

What are the legal arguments that can be used to challenge a state's refusal to sanction gay marriages?

The constitutional arguments most commonly used are that the refusal is a violation of the First-Amendment right of freedom of association, an abridgment of the constitutional right to privacy, and a denial of the constitutional guarantee of equal protection of the laws.[7]

The First Amendment generally protects the rights of individuals to associate with one another, but the right to marry or to engage in sexual relations has, however, not yet been recognized by the Supreme Court to be protected specifically by the First Amendment.[8]

The right of privacy has been more clearly defined by the Supreme Court to guarantee freedom from unwarranted government interference in what has been styled as the individual's zone of privacy. Matters so personal and intimate as decisions whether to use contraceptives or not,[9] or whether to have an abortion or not,[10] have been held to be protected. Similarly, the decision of two people to marry and to choose with whom they wish to have consensual sex and an intimate relationship should be protected against needless government interference.[11]

The Supreme Court has recognized that the right to marry is a fundamental right in the context of miscegenation.[12] The denial of such a right to one group, while allowing it to others, may be said to abridge equal protection of the laws unless a substantial reason may be shown for the difference in treatment.

The reasons commonly advanced to justify the refusals to sanction gay marriages are (1) that the government should try to cure homosexuals and not encourage homosexuality by tolerating and legalizing it; (2) that issuing a marriage license would place states in the anomalous position of officially sanctioning a relationship that may encourage the commission of illegal acts such as sodomy; and (3) that most Americans view marriage as a union between a man and a woman who can consummate a marriage by heterosexual intercourse, and almost the same number believe homosexuality to be morally reprehensible.

Many responses are possible. First, the American Psychiatric Association has concluded that gays are not "sick" and need not be "cured."[13] In any event, prevailing medical opinion has long been that it is almost impossible to change sexual orientation.[14] Second, the laws that prohibit consensual sexual acts in private between adults are probably unconstitutional.[15] Furthermore, many sexual acts are prohibited by law even when they are committed by married heterosexuals. Moreover, there are various sexual acts that may be performed by gays in private that are not proscribed by statute.[16]

Finally, the Bill of Rights was intended, in part, to protect minorities against discriminatory treatment imposed by reason of a majority's deeply felt beliefs. Many Americans believed that interracial marriages were immoral, but the courts have nonetheless held unequivocally that such marriages may not be prohibited.[17] Society's moral preferences, whether based on religion or not, should not permit the denial of a fundamental right.

As noted, no court has yet accepted these arguments.

Personal Finances

May two gays enter into the equivalent of a marriage contract, enforceable in court, by executing an agreement to define their domestic rights and obligations?

Many persons entering into marriage have in recent years executed contracts defining their domestic rights and obligations toward each other. Such contracts may include provisions regarding such matters as dishwashing, cooking, cleaning, and child care. We doubt that such provisions are intended to be, or could be, enforceable in the courts. Instead, they are presumably intended merely to set forth, for the private guidance of the parties, the outlines of their mutual obligations. Gays, if they wish to do so, could lawfully create similar guidelines for themselves.

May gays intending to live together, enter into a contract setting forth their financial obligations toward each other? Will such an agreement be enforceable?

Traditionally, the law has been reluctant to recognize agreements between two unmarried people that purport to establish a financial relationship similar to that of a married couple, unless the agreements are made in anticipation of marriage. Such agreements have been viewed as undermining marriage as an institution. Indeed, in the eyes of some judges, agreements of this kind are akin to prostitution—establishing a scheme under which one or both partners provide sexual services in return for money or other material benefits.

In 1976, in a famous case involving the actor, Lee Marvin,[18] the California Supreme Court overturned this common-law rule—and made headlines from coast-to-coast—by holding that a property agreement between two unmarried adults who live together and engage in sexual relations, is fully enforceable in a court of law (except, as the court put it, "to the extent that the contract is *explicitly* founded on the consideration of meretricious sexual services"). The court went so far as to declare that the agreement need not be written, and could be implied from the conduct of the parties. This revolutionary decision, establishing a right to what the popular press has delighted in dubbing *palimony*, has since been followed in whole, or in part, by courts in other states, including New York.[19]

The California court's reasoning seems just as applicable to homosexual as to heterosexual couples, and at least one court in California has already issued an opinion that appears to bring gay couples within the compass of *Marvin*.[20] However, the right established in the *Marvin* case is still unsettled and untested. At this primitive stage in the law, any gay couple that attempts to put its financial relationship in order through the use of a *Marvin* agreement takes the risk that a court will refuse to enforce it. The safest course is to undertake protective measures in addition to the agreement—executing wills, trust instruments, powers of attorney, and any other appropriate documents that express your mutual wishes; establishing joint ownership of assets you wish to hold as a couple; and doing anything else you have determined, in consultation with your lawyer, accountant, banker, or investment counselor, to be appropriate to your circumstances.[21]

May two gays enter into joint financial obligations to third parties?

Yes. Many unmarried persons living together sign leases obligating both of them to pay the rent and to assume the other obligations of the lease. Many unmarried persons, whether living together or not, sign notes at banks obligating both of them to pay the amounts due under the loans. Such obligations are termed *joint and several*, which means that the creditor may, at his election, sue either or both of the parties and collect the full amount from either of them.[22] It does not necessarily mean that if the creditor sues one party, and collects the whole amount, the other debtor will escape all liability. Depending on the understanding between them, the debtor who has been required to pay the creditor, may have a right to obtain contribution from the other debtor of a portion of the amount involved.

If two gays are living together, will one be liable for the debts of the other?

Not unless the one who did not incur the debt has undertaken to be responsible for its payment.

Under the laws of most states, a married partner (traditionally the husband only) must assume liability for "necessaries" (food, clothing, and so forth) purchased by the other (traditionally the wife). In addition, when one partner customarily buys items from a particular shop, and the other regularly pays the bills, the shop may be justified in assuming that one acts as agent for the other, and that his or her purchases are made on the credit of the other. In such situations, a husband or wife may be liable for anything that the other purchases.[23] However, when single people are involved, unless one has expressly or implicitly indicated to a third party that the other acts as agent, the person who did not incur the debt, would not be liable.

May two gays own property together?

Certainly. Many persons not married to each other are co-owners of property. There are essentially three forms of co-ownership of property: (1) tenancy in common; (2) joint tenancy with the right of survivorship; and (3) tenancy by the entirety. A tenancy in common means that two or more persons own undivided interests in the same property. If one of the co-owners dies, his estate receives his share of the property, and it is passed to his heirs or legatees. A joint tenancy with the right of survivorship means that two or more persons own undivided interests in the same property, and that upon the death of one of the owners, his or her share passes to the surviving owners. The most common illustration is the joint bank account, which customarily is registered in the form "A or B, payable to either or survivor." If the parties intend to open a joint account, each party is entitled to half of the account while both are living, and upon the death of either, the survivor is entitled to the entire account.

The last form of co-ownership, tenancy by the entirety, is available only to married couples. It is, however, so similar to joint tenancy with the right of survivorship that it cannot be said that unmarried persons suffer any disability. In fact, the most substantial difference may be an advantage for unmarried persons. If one of two or more tenants in common or joint tenancy with the right of survivorship is unhappy with the situation and wishes to terminate the tenancy, he may bring an action in court to "partition" the property. The court will direct the property to be sold, and the proceeds divided among the tenants in accordance with their respective interests. Tenants by the entirety, however, may not bring such an action of partition, and if one party is dissatisfied, he is without remedy until the marriage is dissolved, at which time the tenancy by the entirety is automatically transformed into a tenancy in common, or until one of the parties dies, at which time the survivor takes full rights of ownership.

What is community property, and may two gays hold property as community property?

Community property is a system of ownership of property derived from Spanish law and now used in eight states: Texas, California, Washington, Arizona, Louisiana, Nevada, New Mexico, and Idaho. Under the law of community property, income earned by either married party during the marriage is deemed to be held in "community," and each party owns half. Property earned prior to the marriage, and property acquired during the marriage by gift, bequest, devise, or inheritance is not part of the "community" and is the "separate" property of the spouse earning or receiving it. Since community property applies only to married couples, two gays living together will not be affected by it.

If two gays are living together, is there any legal obligation to support each other?

No. There are no laws requiring unmarried persons living together to support each other.

Do two gays living together have rights of inheritance from each other?

No. If a person dies without a will, his or her property is distributed in accordance with the intestate statutes of the state in which he or she was domiciled (a permanent resident) at the time of death. Such statutes commonly provide that the decedent's estate will be distributed to his or her surviving spouse or descendants in varying shares. If there is no surviving spouse or descendants, the estate is usually distributed to the parents of the deceased; or, if they are not living, to the brothers and sisters of the deceased; or, if none are living, to nephews and nieces of the deceased, and so on to more distant relatives.[24]

May gay persons living together name each other as beneficiaries in their wills?
Yes.

Would the will be subject to challenge by blood relations?
Every will is subject to challenge by persons interested in the estate. In general, wills are subject to challenge on the following grounds: (1) improper execution[25]; (2) lack of mental competency of the testator;[26] (3) undue influence[27]; and (4) fraud.[28]

The probable ground for contesting such a will would be that the testator had been unduly influenced in the preparation and execution of the will. Undue influence has been defined as physical coercion or threats of physical harm and duress, or influence so potent as to overpower the will of the testator and subject it to the will and control of another.[29] Undue influence does not exist merely because there is a relationship of affection or friendship between the parties.[30] To the contrary, such a relationship is a circumstance favorable to sustaining a will.[31] A person is entitled to bequeath his property to whomever he desires, and nothing is more natural than to bequeath one's property to one for whom one has an emotional fondness. Moreover, that a person is said to have ingratiated himself with another in order to encourage a bequest is not cause for upsetting a will.[32]

Nonetheless, despite these general rules, undue influence is ultimately a question of fact to be decided by a judge or jury. It is possible that a judge or jury might consider an affectionate relationship between gays so improper as to constitute undue influence.[33]

What may be done to avoid any possible challenge to such a will?
Every possible step should be taken to provide evidence that the will is the independent choice of the testator. The

testator should, for example, consult an attorney with no business or other relationship with the proposed beneficiary. The testator should explain the matter fully to the attorney. At a minimum, he should acquaint the lawyer with the extent of his assets, and the identity of the relatives whom he is excluding from the will. The reason for this is that one of the prerequisites for establishing competence to make a will, is that the testator knew the extent of his estate. The testator should ask his attorney to make a memorandum of such information.

If a gay relationship is of long standing, the parties might consider drawing up a new will periodically without destroying the prior versions. The repetition will itself provide evidence of the testator's seriousness of purpose, and those interested in contesting the will, may be deterred by the fact that even if they are successful in contesting the last will, they will also have to contest each of the earlier versions.

If a gay person fails to provide for another by will, would the survivor have any recourse against the deceased's estate?

No, unless such a right had been created by contract.

May an umarried person recover damages for the wrongful death of another unmarried person?

No. Almost every state has provided by statute that a surviving spouse or other family member may recover damages from those responsible for the accidental death of a husband, wife, or child. No such right has been given to unmarried people.

May a gay person purchase life insurance on his or her own life, and name anyone as beneficiary?

Yes. There are no legal restrictions on the purchase of life insurance by a gay person, and none on the persons whom she or he may designate as beneficiary. It has, however, been suggested that insurance companies may hesitate to issue policies to those who wish to name as beneficiaries those with whom the insureds have "meretricious" relationships. One solution that has been used is to purchase a policy naming the insured's estate as beneficiary, reserve the right to change the beneficiary, and thereafter change the beneficiary.

May gays purchase life insurance on each other?

In order to purchase life insurance, the applicant must have an "insurable interest" in the life of the person to be insured.[34] The rule is obviously intended to avoid inducements for homicide, and to prevent unlawful wagering contracts. In New York, for example, the term *insurable interest* means (a) in the case of persons related closely by blood or law, a substantial interest engendered by love and affection; and (b) in the case of other persons, a lawful and substantial economic interest in having the life, health, or bodily safety of the insured continue.[35] The statutes of other states are generally comparable.

Any question of insurable interest may be avoided by having the insured purchase the insurance on his own life, designating the other as beneficiary. If the insured wants to be certain that the insurance will not be taxed for estate-tax purposes upon death, he or she may assign ownership of the policy to the beneficiary. In this way, although the beneficiary may be forbidden to purchase the policy, he or she may ultimately obtain ownership. If the relationship between the insured and the beneficiary continues, the arrangement may be convenient for both.

Will the next of kin of the insured person have a right to contest the beneficiary designation in the same manner as they could contest a will?

No. Insurance policies are governed by the law of contracts, and not by the laws pertaining to wills. An insurance policy is a contract between the insured and the company, whereby the company agrees to pay a third party the proceeds of the policy upon the death of the insured.

Are automobile insurance rates and homeowner's insurance rates higher for unmarried people?

Yes. Automobile insurers and home insurers use marital status as a premium-rating criterion. Single people generally are looked upon as poor risks by insurers, employers, landlords, and those who extend credit, because they are viewed as relatively unstable, pleasure oriented, and rootless. Married people, on the other hand, are viewed as relatively stable, job oriented, and nonmobile.

In 1973, a survey of insurers was done by the Law Student

Division of the American Bar Association, to ascertain the differences in rates for married and unmarried people.[36] It was found that automobile insurance may cost between 25 percent more (for singles over 25), to 40 percent more (for singles under 25) than for married people.[37] Many insurers refuse to sell homeowners' or tenants' insurance to singles living alone or together. If they do, the rates for singles are higher than for married people.[38]

What may be done about such unequal rates?

Some states, including California, Wisconsin, and Illinois, specifically forbid insurance carriers from discriminating on the basis of sexual orientation,[39] or marital status,[40] but even in those states, carriers may usually impose unequal rates if they can show some actuarial basis for them. Most states have done nothing to protect single people against unequal rates.

Automobile insurers and homeowner insurers are private companies and, without statute or administrative regulation, cannot be forced by the courts to treat all citizens even-handedly.

May one gay person name another as a beneficiary of pension proceeds that are payable upon death?

Generally, yes. Pension plans are essentially insurance agreements for the payment of money upon retirement or death. The terms of pension plans vary widely. They are tailored to the needs of the group participating in the plan. It is not common for such plans to limit the persons who may be named as beneficiaries, although plans for state employees occasionally limit beneficiaries to family members.

Are unmarried people living together eligible for family rates in nongovernmental medical insurance plans such as Blue Cross and Blue Shield?

Generally, no. *Families* are usually defined as married people and their children.

It should be added, however, that a few employers now offer their workers insurance policies that cover unmarried partners as well as spouses and children.

What is the difference in federal-income-tax treatment between married persons and unmarried people living together and sharing expenses?

Under present law, the rates for single people (whether living together or not) are actually lower than those for married people. By virtue of a recent change in the Internal Revenue Code, married people are entitled to a special deduction to make up for the discrepancy in rates, provided that both partners work, and file a joint return.[41]

The joint return in itself gives married people a major advantage over the nonmarried. Joint returns allow married couples to pool their income for purposes of paying tax, and also to pool their deductions, their credits, their gains, and their losses. In the case of a marriage in which one spouse has an income that is much higher than the other's, the right to file a joint return can substantially reduce that spouse's tax liability. Where one partner has capital gains, and the other has capital losses, the two may be offset on a joint return. These benefits are denied single people who live together, who must file separate returns.

Do unmarried persons suffer any disadvantages under the federal estate tax?

Yes. That portion of a decedent's estate that passes to a surviving spouse, is not subject to any estate tax at all.[42] This is referred to as the "marital deduction," and is not available to single people.

Do unmarried persons suffer any disadvantages under the federal gift tax?

Yes. The federal-gift-tax scheme, like the estate-tax scheme, includes a "marital deduction" for transfers to spouses. Under the gift-tax "marital deduction," a wife may give her husband (or a husband his wife) a gift of any size, totally tax free.[43]

Moreover, under the Internal Revenue Code, as revised in 1981, a person may make a gift of up to $10,000 to anyone else in any one year without having to pay gift tax.[44] The code also provides that a spouse may allow half of any gift made by the other spouse to be deemed a gift of the consenting spouse.[45] Thus, a husband may give $20,000 and if the wife consents, each will be deemed to have made a gift of $10,000, and neither will have to pay gift tax.

How may estate taxes be minimized when two unmarried persons live together, and one wishes to leave property to the other upon death?

Various methods may be used, but you should consult a qualified lawyer.

Are there tax disadvantages under the state law for unmarried persons?

The law of each state is different, but most states have provisions similar to the federal statutes described above, with similar consequences for single people.

Government Benefits

Are there government benefits that are available to married people, but are denied to single people who are living together and sharing expenses?

Yes. Some federal and state government benefits such as medical insurance for the aged, and unemployment insurance, may be collected only by the person who qualifies for the benefit. There are, however, other programs such as social security, veterans' benefits, and some disability insurance, in which benefits may be paid to certain family members after the insured's death. The law specifically excludes all others, and even limits the instances in which family members may receive such benefits.[46]

May unmarried persons living together who otherwise qualify, participate in the Food Stamp Program?

Yes. The Food Stamp Program provides, that any "household" that satisfies the financial criteria, may qualify to receive food stamps.[47] The pertinent statute originally provided that a household could qualify only if all members of the household were related by blood or marriage. The limitation was evidently intended to discourage "hippy communes." The Supreme Court of the United States held in *United States Department of Agriculture* v. *Moreno*,[48] that the limitation was impermissible because it was unrelated to the purpose for which the law was adopted—to provide food at a relatively low cost for needy persons. Marital status is not necessarily related to need. The court found that unrelated persons may elect to live together and to pool their resources. It did not, however, hold that all discrimination on the basis of marital status is unconstitutional.[49]

May a person be denied welfare on the basis of homosexuality?
The answer would seem to be no, although there are no reported cases.

May a gay parent receive welfare?
A gay parent who has custody of his or her child, may receive assistance from the state under the Aid to Dependent Children (ADC) program.[50]

May the state deprive a gay parent of welfare on the basis of homosexual conduct?
Almost certainly no.[51]

Must the income of other adults in a household be taken into account in determining a family's financial need?
No. In determining need for ADC, the state may not assume that a person who is not legally bound to support a child is in fact doing so. It must have proof that that person is actually contributing to the household.[52]

Child Custody and Visitation Rights

Until recently, and with good reason, few gay parents—even those already separated or divorced—were willing to reveal their homosexuality for fear that they would jeopardize their rights as parents. Traditionally, American courts, and child welfare agencies as well, have been totally unsympathetic to gay parents, accepting without question, the historic prejudice against gay people, and often relying on facile, outmoded, and unsupportable theories about what happens to children who grow up in homosexual households.

Since 1970, however, the prospects for gay parents have improved considerably. In a significant number of recent cases, judges faced with custody issues involving a gay parent, have shown an open-mindedness that was almost completely absent fifteen years ago.

This section is concerned basically with two rights—the right to custody, and the right to visitation. The right to custody is simply the right to live with, and care for, a child. The right arises automatically at the birth of a child, and continues until the child comes of age or leaves home, unless certain events intervene that eventually lead a court to order a termination of custody.

The right to visitation is the right of a parent who does not have custody of his or her child, to see the child for brief periods of time, one night a week perhaps, or weekends or holidays. The precise times of visitation are generally set forth in a court order, although they may be determined by a separation agreement between the mother and father or in another document.

When may challenges to child custody arise?

Custody questions are most likely to arise in connection with a divorce, or a separation prior to a divorce. Every divorce must be officially granted by order of a court. Customarily, when couples divorce, the court decides which parent will have custody of the children, and what the visitation rights of the other parent will be.

A parent may confront challenges to custody even after this has been awarded. If one parent only discovers that the other is gay after the divorce and custody are granted, he or she may go back to the court and seek custody of children on the basis of the other's homosexuality.

No custody order is truly final. Courts are generally given wide discretion to protect the children brought before them, and they have continuing authority until the children leave the jurisdiction or reach majority. If a court believes that it would be best to remove custody from a parent, it may do so at any time. Moreover, custody questions may be reopened in any state in which the children reside. If, for example, the original custody order was issued in New York, and the mother thereafter moves to Arizona with her child, any suit by interested persons wishing to challenge her custody on the basis of "changed circumstances," may do so in the Arizona courts. The Arizona court is not bound by the New York order, but it is unlikely to alter the order if there are no new circumstances that were unknown to the New York court at the time the order was issued.

What should a parent do if custody rights are challenged?

Obtain the help of a lawyer. You are entitled to a hearing to determine whether you should have custody of your children. If you cannot afford a lawyer, some courts will appoint a lawyer or you can consult a local legal-aid society, community legal-services office, or other law group that provides free or inexpensive legal services. Be certain that the lawyer is sympathetic to the rights of gay parents to have custody of their children. You can contact a local gay organization, listed in Appendix E, for the names of lawyers who have handled such cases before, or are sympathetic to the issue. It is important to be open with your lawyer about the fact that you are gay so that you may explore the lawyer's feelings about your right to custody, and also so that the lawyer will be prepared to defend your rights.

What is the law governing custody and visitation?

The standard for determining questions of custody and visitation in a divorce or separation proceeding, is the "best interests" of the child. Obviously, this standard gives a judge extraordinary latitude; virtually anything deemed relevant to the child's welfare, including a parent's sexuality, can be taken into consideration. It also permits a narrow-minded or unsophisticated judge to indulge prejudices about unorthodox behavior.

The standard is somewhat stricter in neglect proceedings. A neglect proceeding is when the state brings legal action against a parent, alleging that a child has been neglected and should be placed in the custody of someone else, or of the state. It generally arises only when the family has come to the attention of a state social worker, usually because the parent has been receiving public assistance, or has a criminal record. In neglect proceedings, the state must show that the parent is an unfit custodian, and the child has, or will, suffer harm as a result.[53]

Whatever the appropriate standard, it is clear that any parent whose custody has been challenged is entitled under the U.S. Constitution to a full and fair hearing of the allegations against him or her.[54]

Have the courts upheld the rights of gays to be granted custody of their children?

As already indicated, most courts regrettably have not.

However, there is clearly a trend toward a greater acceptance of gay parents.

This excerpt from a 1976 Ohio opinion demonstrates the degree to which homophobic sentiments continue to motivate some judges:

> There is no question in the court's mind, of course, that society as a whole disapproves of sexual aberration of any kind, particularly homosexualism *[sic]*, and that is a very ancient disapproval. You read in the Old Testament of Sodom and Gomorrah. . . . An overwhelming majority of the people in this country strongly disapprove of homosexualism *[sic]*, regard it as a very wide aberration from what they do approve as indicated by various cant appellations they give to it, such as "Queer," "Faggot," and so forth, so there can be no question in the court's mind that the conduct revealed here is against the mores of our present day society, even this society that grows more permissive.[55]

The judge in this case concluded that the mother was unfit because she had "boldly and brazenly se[t] up in the home where the children are to be reared, the lesbian practices which have been current there, clearly to the neglect of supervision of the children."[56]

What are examples of cases in which gays have been denied custody?

The number of reported cases on this issue is small. Few of the disputes over custody or visitation ever reach trial, and even in those cases, officially reported opinions are rare, in part because access to matrimonial and juvenile records is often restricted in deference to the privacy rights of the parties involved.

Here is an assortment of recent cases in which gay parents have been denied custody:

• In a Georgia decision in 1973,[57] the court awarded custody of a nine-year-old girl to the paternal grandparents because of the mother's unorthodox life-style, which the court said included smoking marijuana and teaching the child about "the gay life." The father had indicated that he felt his former wife should retain custody, and a psychiatrist had testified that the child was well adjusted, properly cared for, and exposed to much love and affection.

• In a California decision handed down that same year,[58] a juvenile court ordered that four children be placed in a foster home because of their mother's lesbianism. An appeals court upheld the order, in part because "[t]he continuous existence of a homosexual relationship in the home where the minor is exposed to it involved the necessary likelihood of serious adjustment problems." The mother attempted to regain the children a year later in another proceeding, but was once again rebuffed.

• In a New York case in 1976,[59] the court ordered a change of custody from the mother to the father, even though the mother had cared for the child for the seven years since the separation, because a "home environment with [a] homosexual partner in residence is not a proper atmosphere in which to bring up this child or in the best interest of this child." The court also severely circumscribed the mother's visitation rights, forbidding her to keep the child overnight, or to see her in the company of any other gay person.

• In a Colorado opinion handed down in 1980,[60] the mother of two children, aged ten and four, was denied custody even though two of the three testifying experts had indicated that she would be the better custodian. The judge pronounced both mother and father "fit and proper parents," but stated, "I think that the problem of the homosexuality of the mother is severe now, with the oldest child being ten and can't help but become more severe as the children go into puberty, adolescence, and an effort is made to raise the children." The judge failed to specify what he meant by "the problem of the homosexuality of the mother."

What are examples of cases in which the courts have sustained the custody rights of gay people?

• In a Michigan neglect proceeding in the early 1970s,[61] an appeals court overturned a probate court order in which the six children of two lesbian mothers who had been living together, were placed in foster homes. The court declared, "There was sufficient evidence to support the conclusion that the women were engaged in a lesbian relationship. However, there is very little to support the conclusion that this relationship rendered the home an unfit place for the children to reside." This is apparently the first reported case in which a court permitted a gay couple to keep their children and continue to live together.

• In what is perhaps the most famous lesbian custody case,[62] after a trial with twenty-one witnesses, including eleven psychiatrists and psychologists, two lesbian women were allowed to continue to live together with their eight children. It found that splitting them up into two households would be a hardship on the children, and therefore not in their best interests. On appeal, the Washington Supreme Court upheld that portion of the order allowing the mothers to retain custody, but ordered them to live separately.

• In a Maine opinion of 1976,[63] the court awarded full custody to a lesbian mother without any conditions, but crucial to its conclusion was its inference that the mother was "intelligently seeking to minimize, if not totally eliminate" the impact of her homosexuality on her children, which presumably meant that she was generally quiet about her sexual orientation.

• In a Colorado neglect proceeding in 1977,[64] the court awarded custody to the lesbian lover of the children's mother, who had committed suicide. The couple had lived together with the children for thirteen years. The alternative would have been to award custody to the mother's sister and brother-in-law.

In many cases, a court will award custody or visitation rights only under certain conditions. The parent might be forbidden to live with her lover, or even to be with the children in her lover's presence.[65] She may only be allowed to see the child in the presence of another nonhomosexual adult.[66]

Can homosexuality per se be grounds for denying custody or visitation rights?

Several courts have now declared explicitly, that it is improper to deny custody or visitation rights to a parent merely on the ground of homosexuality.[67] There must be proof that the children are actually harmed by their parent's homosexuality. Of course, there are some judges who infer that harm is being inflicted on the child simply because a parent leads a life that is unconventional, but a recent Supreme Court opinion[68] indicates that inferences of this kind may be a violation of the constitutional guarantee of due process of law.

How can a gay parent prove to a court that he or she is a proper custodian?

It is generally useful in custody cases to have both the children and parents examined by a qualified psychiatrist or psychologist. If possible, this should be done with the consent of the court prior to the hearing. The psychiatrist may be able to testify at the hearing that the parent is a stable and good parent, and that the children will not be adversely affected by exposure to a homosexual parent or the parent's lover.

A common question doctors are asked at custody hearings, is whether it is likely that the child will become a homosexual if he or she continues to live or visit with the gay parent (which the court ordinarily concludes is a negative result, given society's disapproval). Doctors are also commonly asked whether the child is overly anxious about the parent's homosexuality—that is, embarrassed or distressed by it. Sometimes doctors are even asked whether there is any likelihood that the child will be molested by either the parent or the parent's gay friends.

You should try to be examined by a doctor who has actually done research in the field of homosexuality, and who is sympathetic to the problems of a gay parent. Local gay organizations often keep lists of such doctors.

Will a gay parent be compelled to testify about the details of his or her sexual activities?

In custody cases, the court is entitled to have information regarding all aspects of the parents' behavior in order to ascertain whether such behavior is in the best interests of the child. Despite the latitude given courts in collecting such information, however, you may not be compelled to provide detailed information regarding your sexual activities. First, if sodomy is a crime in the state in which you reside, you may be able to refuse to answer any questions about your sexual activity on the ground that it might incriminate you. Second, the constitutional right of privacy prevents inquiries into private sexual activities, unless there is a compelling state interest to do so. You should not be forced to answer such questions unless the state or the challenging person first shows how those activities may affect the welfare of your child.

What are the constitutional arguments that may be asserted so that gay parents can gain custody of their children?

The right of parents to have and raise children has been deemed by the Supreme Court to be "essential to the orderly pursuit of happiness by free men,"[69] "one of the basic civil rights of man,"[70] and "far more precious . . . than property rights."[71] The only legitimate justification the state may have for interfering with the parent-child relationship, is to protect the welfare of the child. If the state attempts to remove a child from the home because of parental conduct, it has the burden of proving that the conduct renders the parent "so unfit as to endanger the child's welfare."[72]

It may also be argued that a court violates a parent's right to privacy if it makes private sexual conduct the focus of its decision without a demonstration that such conduct adversely affects the children. It may be further argued that a denial of custody to a gay parent infringes the constitutional guarantee of equal protection.

Adoption and Foster Care

May a gay person adopt a child?

The laws of many states permit a single person to be an adoptive parent, and no state expressly prohibits adoption by gays. Adoption of children by gays is, however, still controversial. A court must first find that the "best interests" of the child will be served by the adoption.

If the question of fitness arises, a gay person should insist that a hearing be held on the question. Expert psychiatric testimony should be obtained, and a psychiatric evaluation of the child should be made to determine whether the homosexuality of the potential parent would have any adverse effect on the child.

In a recent case in New York State, a man was permitted to retain permanent custody of a thirteen-year-old boy he had adopted a year previously, even though he had subsequently declared publicly that he was gay, and was living with another man. The judge reportedly stated:

> I saw no reason why this adoption should not be permanent. I'm not just trying to get into new avenues. I'm just trying to deal with this one matter before me. I assume some people will be criticial, but look at it this way: the man doesn't beat his son, and when you look at all the cases of child abuse you get from so-called straights, you grasp for words. [73]

May a gay adult adopt another adult? What are the advantages? What are the disadvantages?

Most states allow the adoption of an adult, so long as the person to be adopted, and his or her natural parents (if alive and known) grant their consent. However, as with children, a court must approve the adoption.

In one of the first cases of its kind in the country, an appellate court in New York recently approved a petition by a thirty-two-year-old male to adopt his forty-three-year-old lover. The petition made clear that a prime motive behind the attempted adoption was the fear that the two might be evicted from their rented apartment, since only the older man had signed the lease, and the lease contained a clause limiting occupancy to members of the tenant's immediate family. The court held this motive no bar to the adoption, noting that "[a]doption is often utilized by adults for strictly economic purposes, especially inheritance." The court also pointed out that New York's highest court had recently invalidated the state's prohibition on consensual sodomy. The court then declared:

> The "nuclear family" arrangement is no longer the only model of family life in America. The realities of present day urban life allow many different types of non-traditional families. The statutes involved do not permit this court to deny a petition for adoption on the basis of this court's view of what is the nature of a family. [74]

Even if most courts do eventually accept the reasoning of the New York court, the step of adopting another adult should be approached with great caution. An adoption is forever; it creates a virtually indissoluble legal link between "parent" and "child." Moreover, it may give rise to substantial liabilities on the part of the adopting parent. In many states, an adopting parent is responsible for the financial support of the person adopted, at least under circumstances of extreme need. In addition, in some states, he or she may be guilty of incest for engaging in sexual relations with the "child."[75]

Furthermore, the financial benefits of adoption are usually minimal. Many government benefits for parents are available only if the child is under eighteen.[76] One court has even indicated that a parent is not entitled to government benefits for an adopted child, regardless of age, if the adoption was made for the purpose of monetary gain.[77]

May a gay person qualify as a foster parent?

In a number of states, gay people have been permitted to become foster parents to gay children. Some gay organizations have been working with child welfare and placement agencies to permit such arrangements. Check with your local gay organization or child-welfare agency for information.

In general, state agencies have been more reluctant to place children with gay males than with lesbians.[78]

NOTES

1. TEX. FAM. CODE ANN., §1.01.
2. Reynolds v. United States, 98 U.S. 244 (1879).
3. Baker v. Nelson, 291 Minn. 310, 191 N.W. 2d 185 (1971), *appeal dismissed*, 409 U.S. 810 (1972). See also Adams v. Howerton, 486 F. Supp. 1119 (C.D. Cal. 1980), supporting a refusal by the Immigration and Naturalization Service to recognize the validity of a same-sex marriage in Colorado.
4. Jones v. Hallahan, 501 S.W. 2d 588 (Ky. Ct. App. 1973).
5. Singer v. Hara, 11 Wash. App. 247, 522 P.2d 1187 (1974).
6. No state need recognize a contract entered into in another country that would violate its own public policy.
7. See generally Note, *The Legality of Homosexual Marriage*, 82 Yale L. J. 573 (1973); Rivera, *Our Straight-Laced Judges: The Legal Position of Homosexual Persons in the United States*, 30 Hastings L. J. 799, 874–78 (1979); Comment, *Homosexuals' Right to Marry: A*

Constitutional Test and a Legislative Solution, 128 U. Pa. L. Rev. 193 (1979).

8. The First Amendment, as construed by the Supreme Court, includes a number of other rights, among them the right to engage in free and private associations. Williams v. Rhodes, 393 U.S. 23 (1968); NAACP v. Alabama, 357 U.S. 449 (1958). Most right of association cases to date have dealt with association for political purposes, although in Griswold v. Connecticut, 381 U.S. 479, 484 (1965), Justice Douglas refers to marriage as an "association."

9. Griswold v. Connecticut, *supra* note 8; Eisenstadt v. Baird, 405 U.S. 438 (1972).

10. Roe V. Wade, 410 U.S. 113 (1973).

11. See generally Barnett, *Sexual Freedom and the Constitution* (1973).

12. Loving v. Virginia, 388 U.S. 1 (1967). See also Zablocki v. Redhail, 434 U.S. 374 (1978).

13. Resolution of the American Psychiatric Association issued Dec. 15, 1973.

14. See, e.g. Bell, Weinberg, and Hammersmith, *Sexual Preference: Its Development in Men and Women* (1981); Karlen, *Sexuality and Homosexuality* (1971), 572–606; Report of the Committee on Homosexual Offenses and Prostitution ¶¶ 17, 25–30 (1957) [Wolfenden Report].

15. See, e.g. People v. Onofre, 51 N.Y. 2d 476, 434 N.Y.S. 2d 947, 415 N.E. 2d 936 (1980), *cert. denied*, 451 U.S. 987 (1981), discussed in chapter IX of this book.

16. See Barnett, *supra* note 11.

17. See Loving v. Virginia, *supra* note 12.

18. Marvin v. Marvin, 18 Cal. 3d 660, 557 P.2d 106, 134 Cal. Rptr. 815 (1976).

19. Morone v. Morone, 50 N.Y. 2d 481, 429 N.Y.S. 2d 592, 407 N.E. 2d 438 (1980). See also Beal v. Beal, 4 Fam. L. Rptr. (BNA) 2464 (Ore. 1978); Carlson v. Olson, 3 Fam. L. Rptr. (BNA) 2467 (Minn. 1977). But see Hewitt v. Hewitt, 48 U.S.L.W. 2223 (Ill. Sup. Ct., Sept. 19, 1979), in which the Illinois Supreme Court explicitly rejected the Marvin approach.

20. See Jones v. Daly, 122 Cal. App.3d 500, 176 Cal. Rptr. 130 (1981); see also Rivera, *supra* note 7, at 905, n. 640. There are now reports of similar cases throughout the country. See *National Law Journal*, May 18, 1981, p. 1. See generally Kay and Amyx, *Marvin v. Marvin: Preserving the Options*, 65 Cal. L. Rev. 937, 967–68 (1977); comment, 90 Harv. L. Rev. 1708, 1719 (1977).

21. See generally *The Law & Our Personal Lives* (1978), published by the Lambda Legal Defense & Education Fund, Inc., 132 W. 43 St. New York, NY 10036; "Legal Planning for Loving Partnerships," in *Our Right to Love—A Lesbian Resource Book*, 216–19 (1978).

22. See, e.g. Rice v. Gove, 22 Pick. 158 (Mass. 1839).

23. See, e.g. Wanamaker v. Weaver, 176 N.Y. 75, 68 N.E. 135 (1903).

24. See, e.g. NEW YORK ESTATES, POWERS, AND TRUSTS LAW §4–1.1.
25. See, e.g. Freiders v. Freiders, 180 Wisc. 430, 193 N.W. 77 (1923).
26. See, e.g. Delafield v. Parish, 25 N.Y. 9 (1862).
27. See, e.g. Marx v. McGlynn, 88 N.Y. 358 (1882).
28. See, e.g. Burney v. Torrey, 100 Ala. 157, 14 So. 685 (1893).
29. Marx v. McGlynn, *supra* note 27, at 370–72.
30. See, e.g. Matter of Brand, 185 App. Div. 134, 173 N.Y.S. 169 (3d Dept. 1918); Matter of Dunn, 184 App. Div. 386, 171 N.Y.S. 1056 (3d Dept. 1918).
31. See, e.g. Matter of Fleischmann, 176 App. Div. 785, 163 N.Y.S. 426 (2nd Dept. 1917).
32. See, e.g. Matter of Brand, *supra* note 30.
33. Cf. Matter of Kaufmann, 20 A.D. 2d 464, 247 N.Y.S. 2d 664 (1st Dept. 1964), *aff'd*, 15 N.Y. 2d 825, 257 N.Y.S. 2d 941, 205 N.E. 2d 864 (1965). See generally Sherman, *Undue Influence and the Homosexual Testator*, 42 U. Pitts. L. Rev. 225 (1981).
34. Cross v. National Fire Insurance Co., 132 N.Y. 133, 30 N.E. 390 (1892).
35. NEW YORK INSURANCE LAW, §146(2).
36. Coleman, *Unmarried Person's Bill of Rights*, Report to the Law Student Division of the American Bar Association (Jan. 1973).
37. *Id.* at 9.
38. *Id.* at 10.
39. See discussion in Rivera, *supra* note 7, at 906.
40. See, e.g. NEW YORK INSURANCE LAW, §40–e.
41. 26 U.S.C. §221.
42. 26 U.S.C. §2056.
43. 26 U.S.C. §2523.
44. 26 U.S.C. §2503(b).
45. 26 U.S.C. §2513.
46. See generally *The Catalogue of Federal Domestic Assistance* (Office of Management and Budget, Washington, D.C.), for a guide to what federal benefits are available. The catalogue is updated regularly.
47. 7 U.S.C. §2011, *et seq*.
48. 413 U.S. 528 (1973).
49. See the discussion of Moreno and subsequent Supreme Court cases in chapter VII of this book.
50. 42 U.S.C. §601, *et seq*.
51. See generally King v. Smith, 392 U.S. 309 (1968) (overturning an Alabama regulation denying ADC payments to children whose mother "cohabits" with a man).
52. See Lewis v. Martin, 397 U.S. 552 (1970).
53. Rivera, *supra* note 7, at 883–904, contains an excellent and comprehensive discussion of the law surrounding custody and visitation rights for gay parents. (The Rivera article has been updated in Rivera, *Recent Developments in Sexual Preference Law*, 30 Drake L. Rev. 311 (1980–81).) See also Hunter and Polikoff, *Custody Rights of*

Lesbian Mothers: Legal Theory and Litigation, 25 Buff. L. Rev. 691 (1976); Lauerman, *Non-Marital Sexual Conduct and Child Custody,* 46 U. Cin. L. Rev. 647, 649 (1977). Also helpful is Sussman and Guggenheim, *The Rights of Parents,* an ACLU handbook published in 1980, which contains a chapter on gay parents.

54. See Stanley v. Illinois, 405 U.S. 645 (1972).

55. Towend v. Towend, No. 639 (Ohio Ct. App., Portage County, Sept. 30, 1976), quoted in Rivera, *supra* note 7, at 902.

56. *Id.*

57. Bennett v. Clemens, 230 Ga. 317, 196 S.E. 2d 842 (1973).

58. In re Tammy F., 1 Civ. No. 32648 (Cal. App., Aug. 21, 1973), *petition for hearing denied,* Nov. 7, 1973, reported in Women's Rights L. Rptr. 19 (1974), and described in Rivera, *supra* note 7, at 887–88.

59. In re Jane B., 85 Misc. 2d 515, 380 N.Y.S. 2d 848 (Sup. Ct. 1976).

60. Mueller v. Mueller, Civ. Action No. 79–DR–1246 (Colo. Dist. Ct. Jefferson County, Mar. 27, 1980).

61. People v. Brown, 49 Mich. App. 358, 212 N.W. 2d 55 (1973).

62. The case is in fact, two companion cases, Schuster v. Schuster and Isaacson v. Isaacson, Nos. D–36837, D–36868 (Wash. Super. Ct., King County, Dec. 22, 1974), *aff'd in part,* 585 P.2d 130 (1978), discussed in Rivera, *supra* note 7, at 899–90.

63. Whitehead v. Black, Nos. CV–76–422, CV–76–426 (Me. Super. Ct., Cumberland County, June 14, 1976), discussed in Rivera *supra* note 7, at 900.

64. In re Hatzopoulos, Colo., Juv. Ct., Denver County, July 8, 1977, reported in Fam. L. Rptr. 2076 (1977).

65. See, e.g. Mitchell v. Mitchell, No. 240665 (Cal. Super. Ct., Santa Clara County, June 8, 1972), discussed in Rivera, *supra* note 7, at 892–93.

66. See, e.g. Nadler v. Nadler, No. 177331 (Cal. Sup. CT. Sacramento County Nov. 15, 1967).

67. See, e.g. Doe v. Doe, 222 Va. 736, 284 S.E. 2d 799 (1981); Bezio v. Patenaude, 410 N.E. 2d 1207 (Mass. 1980); Nadler v. Superior Court, 255 Cal. App. 2d 523, 63 Cal Rpts. 352 (1967), M.P. v. S.P., 169 N.J. Super. 425, 404 A.2d 1256 (App. Div. 1979).

68. Stanley v. Illinois, 405 U.S. 645 (1972).

69. Meyer v. Nebraska, 262 U.S. 390, 399 (1923).

70. Skinner v. Oklahoma, 316 U.S. 535, 541 (1942).

71. May v. Anderson, 345 U.S. 528, 533 (1953).

72. Washburn v. Washburn, 49 Cal. App. 2d 581, 588, 122 P.2d 96, 100 (1942). See also Santosky v Kramer 102 S.Ct. 1388 (1982).

73. *New York Times,* June 21, 1979, Bl.

74. In re Adult Anonymous II, 452 N.Y.S. 2d 198 (1st Dept. 1982). See also Matter of Adult Anonymous, 106 Misc. 2d 792, 435 N.Y.S. 2d 527 (Fam. Ct., Kings County 1981).

75. For example, in ILL. ANN. STA., ch. 38, §11–10; N.C. GEN. STAT. N.C. §14–178; 18 PA CONS. STA. ANN., §4302; and TEX. FAM. CODE ANN., §2.21.

76. For example, the federal income tax exemption of $1,000 for each dependent is available for a child who is over eighteen, and not a student, only if the child earned less than $1,000 during the year. 26 U.S.C. §151.

77. Craig v. Gardner, 299 F. Supp. 247 (N.D. Tex. 1969), *rev'd on other grounds sub nom.* Craig v. Finch, 425 F.2d 1005 (5th Cir. 1970).

78. *New York Times*, Nov. 27, 1979, B2. Cf. Big Brothers, Inc. v. Minneapolis Commission on Civil Rights, 284 N.W. 2d 823 (Minn. 1979) (Non-profit corporation providing services to boys without fathers may require adult volunteers to disclose sexual orientation and may communicate that information to boys' families, even though city has an antidiscrimination ordinance covering gay people).

IX

Gays and the Criminal Law

There is absolutely nothing unlawful in being gay or lesbian, in and of itself. Homosexuality, that is, the condition of being sexually and emotionally oriented toward persons of the same sex, is a state of being. As such, it cannot constitutionally be considered a crime.[1]

Homosexual orientation, like heterosexual orientation, may or may not lead to specific sexual acts, and at least one court has recognized that there is no basis for the assumption that homosexuals are predisposed to commit a prohibited sexual act.[2] In much of the country, private sexual conduct between consenting adults of the same sex is now lawful. Furthermore, in most states where certain types of sexual conduct are still illegal, there are nonetheless various sexual acts that members of the same sex can engage in without violating the law.

Some courts, however, continue to indulge in the popular myth that "in order to be a homosexual, the prohibited [that is, illegal] act must have at some time been committed or at least presently contemplated."[3] And despite the significant advances in gay rights in recent years, the general public probably still thinks gay people violate the law in their sexual activity.

As of this writing, twenty-five states still criminalize consensual sodomy, and various other sexual acts between consenting homosexual adults. (See Appendix A, which is a state-by-state compilation of the laws applicable to adult gay sexual activity.) Many of these laws also penalize the same conduct when it occurs between members of the opposite sex,[4] but the generalized societal stigma for engaging in such acts does not attach to heterosexuals, as it does to gays.

In addition to the laws concerning sexual conduct, there are other penal statutes that are often enforced against gays, for instance, prohibitions on loitering and solicitation, and sex-offender registration requirements. They will also be discussed in this chapter.

Do legal authorities believe that consensual sexual conduct in private between adults, should be criminalized?

No, quite the contrary. In 1955, the Model Penal Code, a proposed penal code recommended to the states by the prestigious American Law Institute, recommended that all sexual practices not involving force, adult activity with minors, or public conduct, be excluded from the criminal law.[5] In 1957, a specially appointed study committee in Great Britain issued a report, known as the Wolfenden Report, recommending that private adult homosexual conduct be decriminalized.[6] In 1973, the American Bar Association passed a resolution urging the states to repeal all laws that made any form of consenting sexual conduct between adults in private, a criminal act.[7]

How many states have followed the recommendations of these legal authorities and removed criminal penalties for private consensual sexual activity between adults?

Twenty-two states have repealed their consensual sodomy laws by legislation. Those states are Alaska, California, Colorado, Connecticut, Delaware, Hawaii, Illinois, Indiana, Iowa, Maine, Nebraska, New Hampshire, New Jersey, New Mexico, North Dakota, Ohio, Oregon, South Dakota, Vermont, Washington, West Virginia, and Wyoming. The Supreme Court of Florida has declared that state's sodomy law unconstitutional.[8] Florida still has a prohibition against "unnatural and lascivious acts with another person,"[9] which has been interpreted to cover acts formerly prohibited by the sodomy provision.[10] The Massachusetts Supreme Court has ruled that a statute prohibiting unnatural and lascivious acts that had been used to prosecute acts of sodomy and oral copulation, does not apply to private sexual conduct between consenting adults.[11] The high courts of Iowa[12] and Pennsylvania[13] have held that their consensual sodomy laws are inapplicable to private adult consensual conduct, although the Iowa decision was limited to heterosexual conduct. And a federal district court in Texas recently invalidated that state's criminal prohibition on "homosexual conduct."[14] Most importantly, New York's highest court, in a major decision on the constitutionality of sodomy laws, has held that that state's consensual sodomy law is unconstitutional.[15]

Has the United States Supreme Court decided the question of whether state consensual sodomy laws are valid under the Constitution?

No. In one case, *Doe* v. *Commonwealth's Attorney for the City of Richmond*,[16] the Court summarily affirmed, without issuing an opinion, the decision of a lower federal court that upheld the validity of Virginia's sodomy law. However, the legal significance of the court's action in that case is unclear. Some lower courts have concluded that it was a ruling by the court that statutes criminalizing consensual sodomy are valid.[17] Other courts, as well as some commentators, have argued that it has no real precedential value since the court could have had procedural reasons for reaching its decision.[18]

The legal ambiguity on the issue will be resolved only when the Supreme Court confronts it in another case.

On what basis did New York's highest court find that state's statute on consensual sodomy, unconstitutional?

In the absence of a clear statement by the Supreme Court on this important legal question, the 1980 opinion of the New York Court of Appeals in *People* v. *Onofre*,[19] probably stands as the most authoritative guide on the constitutionality of consensual sodomy statutes.

In that opinion, the court traced the Supreme Court's line of cases on the constitutional right to privacy, and concluded that the right covers virtually all "noncommercial, cloistered personal sexual conduct of consenting adults," even "deviant" conduct. It then measured that right against the justifications for the consensual sodomy prohibition put forward by the state—that the statute prevents physical harm, that it promotes "public morality," and that it protects the institution of marriage. The court found that there was no persuasive evidence to support the state's claims, and declared the statute unconstitutional on its face. The court wrote:

> Personal feelings of distaste for the conduct sought to be proscribed . . . and even disapproval by a majority of the populace, if that disapproval were to be assumed, may not substitute for the required demonstration of a valid basis for intrusion by the State in an area of important personal decision protected under the right of privacy drawn from the United States Constitution—areas, the number and definition of which have steadily grown but, as the Supreme Court has observed, the outer limits of which it has not yet marked.[20]

The court of appeals also found the statute constitutionally faulty on another ground. The New York statute distinguished between married and unmarried people; such a distinction also exists in some other states. The law prohibited all acts of anal or oral intercourse, with one exception—two married people with one another. The court held that this distinction was irrational, and therefore a violation of the constitutional guarantee of equal protection of the laws.

What type of sexual conduct between gays is permitted in the states that have either repealed their sodomy laws, or had their laws declared unconstitutional?
Any form of private, consensual sexual conduct among adults is permitted in these states, including oral or anal intercourse, except when done for financial gain.

In the states that still have prohibitions against consensual sodomy, what types of private consensual sexual activity, if any, are legal between gays?
In almost all of these states, both oral and anal intercourse are prohibited, either under the wording of the statutes themselves, or as they have been interpreted by the courts. The Arkansas, Kansas, Kentucky, Missouri, Montana, and Nevada, statutes apply to homosexual conduct only.
The statutes explicitly prohibiting "sodomy" (usually defined as anal or oral sexual intercourse) generally do not prohibit other acts of mutual sexual gratification, such as

mutual masturbation, and those acts would probably be legal in those states, whether between persons of the same sex, or persons of the opposite sex.

A few states, like Maryland, have laws that prohibit "unnatural or perverted sexual practices,"[21] or similarly vaguely worded sexual conduct, in addition to sodomy statutes. Such provisions, while arguably unconstitutional, could, at this stage in the development of the law on gay rights, probably still be used as a justification for arresting gays for *any* form of mutual sexual activity. What you should do if arrested for violating any of these statutes, will be discussed later in this chapter.

Is sexual activity between adults and minors legal?

While many people believe that age restrictions on consensual sexual conduct are too stringent and in need of revision, every jurisdiction continues to maintain some age limit prohibitions with respect to sexual conduct, heterosexual and homosexual alike. The specific age of consent for sexual activities varies from state to state. Generally, a minor will be deemed incapable of consent to sexual activity below a certain age, usually 14 to 16, and severe penalties are prescribed for an adult who engages in sexual conduct with such a minor, even if the minor ostensibly consented. Frequently, the severity of the penalty increases as the age difference between the adult and the minor increases.

Is sexual conduct in public places legal in the states that have repealed their consensual sodomy statutes?

No. Persons engaging in consensual sexual conduct in public places in these states are still subject to arrest under other criminal statutes.

Under what types of statutes are gays subject to arrest for sexual activities in public places?

Generally, there are three classes of statutes under which gays are arrested for sexual activities in public: sodomy, lewd conduct, or other crimes directly concerning sexual conduct; statutes prohibiting certain types of solicitation; and loitering or disorderly conduct statutes.

Sexual conduct in public, whether between gays or heterosexuals, is illegal. While heterosexuals who are apprehended, will often be charged with only disorderly conduct or lewd behavior and escape with a warning, gays are likely to be charged, in addition to disorderly conduct, with violation of the sodomy statutes.

What do solicitation statutes prohibit?

Some states and municipalities have statutes or ordinances that prohibit solicitation of—that is, requesting another person to engage in—conduct that is itself prohibited by law. Thus, where prostitution is illegal, solicitation for prostitution is also usually prohibited.

With respect to gays, solicitation for the purposes of engaging in sexual conduct prohibited by statute, is often made a crime. See Appendix A for a compilation of state laws.

Are solicitation laws valid in states that have repealed prohibitions on private adult consensual sodomy?

Some of the states that have decriminalized consensual sodomy nevertheless retain statutes prohibiting solicitation for such acts. These statutes are subject to legal attack on the grounds that where the conduct itself is legal, it cannot be illegal to ask someone to participate in it, and the highest courts of several states have in fact so ruled.[22]

What are loitering statutes?

Loitering statutes prohibit being or remaining in a public place for no apparent purpose or being in a place for an illegal purpose. Such statutes are subject to legal attack as too vague to inform a person of what conduct is prohibited where they fall into the first category—prohibiting loitering for no apparent purpose.[23] Where they fall into the second category, such as New York's prohibition on loitering for the purpose of "deviate sexual intercourse,"[24] the prosecutor must be able to prove that you were loitering for the illegal purpose.

Even if the case cannot ultimately be proved, however, gay people are still harassed by being arrested under such statutes, frequently in popular cruising places by plainclothes police officers.

What should a gay person do if arrested for an offense related to gay activity?

He should not resist arrest, but he should also not volunteer any information or admit to any conduct to the arresting officer or to any other police officer who may question him about what he was doing. You are not required to give any information other than your name and address. You should refuse to discuss the case further until you have had a chance to talk to a lawyer. You could also contact either a local or state gay organization, or the local or state branch of the ACLU for assistance, or a legal aid or public defender's office.

If charged with an offense related to gay sexual conduct, should you ever agree to plead guilty to a lesser offense such as disorderly conduct?

The question of whether to agree to "cop a plea"—that is, to agree to enter a guilty plea to a lesser offense, if that alternative is offered by the prosecutor or the court, in order to avoid a trial and possible conviction on a greater offense— is a decision that can be made only after the client and his lawyer have carefully evaluated all the facts, including the possible effect on one's employment or occupational status. If one is innocent, and the arrest is groundless, the decision becomes even more difficult because one ordinarily will not want to have an unjustified criminal record.

The question is generally one of proof. Even if innocent, one must consider whether a dishonest police officer, for example, would be likely to lie about what was actually seen in order to obtain a conviction, and whether the judge or jury would be likely to accept the police officer's version of the facts.

What are some of the factors one should consider in determining whether to agree to a guilty plea to a lesser offense?

The primary thing to consider is the type of record that would be established by a conviction on the original charge, and what effect such a record might have on one's future, as opposed to the record that would be created by a plea to a lesser offense, and the likelihood of a conviction on the original charge.

Other factors are whether one has any previous arrests on the same or other charges and how a judge is likely to view them; what penalties are possible on each charge, what publicity might be involved in defending the original charge, and what effect it would have; and what the time involved in defending against the charge would be.

A key consideration is whether one is a member of a licensed trade or profession and what the effect of the possible alternate dispositions would be on one's license. In some states, for example, sodomy is classified as a felony, and conviction of a felony in some licensed professions can mean loss or suspension of a license. In such a case, you should consider carefully with your lawyer whether acceptance of a proffered misdemeanor charge would be the wisest course.

Similarly, some licenses may be revoked or suspended as a result of a conviction on an offense involving "moral turpitude." In such a case, the classification of a crime as a felony or misdemeanor, is less important than whether it is construed as involving moral turpitude. However, several recent cases hold that engaging in homosexual conduct does not, necessarily, make one unfit to hold a license to practice law,[25] or to be a teacher,[26] but these more tolerant views are not yet universally adopted.

Also to be considered is whether a conviction under a particular charge would require registration under "sex offender" statutes in jurisdictions that have them, such as California.

If you decide to contest a charge and plead not guilty, should you seek a jury trial?

This will depend on an evaluation of the facts, a consideration of what is known about the attitudes of the judge likely to try the case, and an appraisal of the attitudes toward gays in the community from which the jurors would probably be selected. If a jury trial is chosen, prospective jurors should be questioned by the defense attorney so as to determine their attitudes toward gays. Jurors who reveal prejudices, should be challenged for cause.

If you win your case, or if the charges against you are dismissed, can you have this arrest removed from your record?

Some states have specific statutory provisions for obtaining fingerprints and photographs in the event charges are dismissed, or you are acquitted. Some states also have provisions for expunging or sealing arrest records in those circumstances. Even when there are no specific statutory provisions for such relief, however, courts are sometimes willing to order a record sealed after a dismissal or acquittal upon motion by the defendant. The possibility should be discussed with your attorney.

What should you do if someone attempts to blackmail you because you are gay?

If you do not know a lawyer with whom you can discuss the matter, contact the local gay organization or ACLU branch. The people there will often have opened channels of communication with the police department so that you would be able to report this. Stall the would-be blackmailer for time until you arrange to contact the police or otherwise receive help. It is almost never advantageous to pay off, since the demands frequently continue and even increase.

NOTES

1. See generally Robinson v. California, 370 U.S. 660 (1962). See also Report of the Committee on Homosexual Offenses and Prostitution Presented to Parliament by the Secretary of State for the Home Department and the Secretary for Scotland by Command of Her Majesty, Sec. 18 (1957) (hereinafter "The Wolfenden Report").
2. People v. Giani, 154 Cal. App. 2d 539, 302 P.2d 813 (1956). See also Gaylord v. Tacoma School District No. 10, 88 Wash. 2d 286, 559 P.2d 1340, 1349 (Dolliver, J., dissenting).
3. Gay Activists Alliance v. Lomenzo, 66 Misc. 2d 456, 320 N.Y.S. 2d 994, 997 (Sup. Ct. 1971), rev'd, 38 A.D. 2d 981, 329 N.Y.S. 2d 181 (3rd Dept. 1972), aff'd, 31 N.Y. 2d 965, 341 N.Y.S. 2d 108 (1973).
4. See, e.g. Lovisi v. Slayton, 539 F.2d 349 (4th Cir.), cert. denied, sub nom. Lovisi v. Zahradnick, 429 U.S. 977 (1976).
5. Model Penal Code, Sec. 207.5(1) Comment (Tent. Draft No. 4 1955).
6. The Wolfenden Report, supra note 1.
7. 42 U.S.L.W. 2098 (Aug. 14, 1973).
8. Franklin v. State, 257 So. 2d 21 (Fla. 1971). The state legislature subsequently repealed the statute (FLA. STAT. ANN. §800.01).
9. FLA. STAT. ANN §800.02.
10. Franklin v. State, supra note 8; Johnsen v. State, 332 So. 2d 69 (1976).
11. Commonwealth v. Balthazar, 366 Mass. 298, 318 N.E. 2d 478 (1974).
12. State v. Pilcher, 242 N.W. 2d 348 (Ia. 1976).
13. Commonwealth v. Bonadio, 490 Pa. 91, 415 A.2d 47 (1980).

14. Baker v. Wade, 51 V.S.L. @ 2149 (N.D. Tex., Aug. 17, 1982).
15. People v. Onofre, 51 N.Y. 2d 476 (1980), 434 N.Y.S. 2d 947, 415 N.E. 2d 936 (1980), *cert. denied*, 451 U.S. 987 (1981).
16. 403 F. Supp. 1199 (E.D. Va. 1975), *aff'd without opinion*, 425 U.S. 901 (1976).
17. See, e.g. Childers v. Dallas Police Dept., 513 F. Supp. 134, 146 (N.D. Tex. 1981); Petition of Nemetz, 485 F. Supp. 470, 471 (E.D. Va. 1980), *rev'd*, 647 F.2d 432 (4th Cir. 1981). See also Beller v. Middendorf, 632 F.2d 788, 809–10 (9th Cir. 1980).
18. See, e.g. People v. Onofre, *supra* note 15, 434 N.Y.S. 2d at 953–54; benShalom v. Secretary of the Army, 489 F. Supp. 964, 976 (E.D. Wisc. 1980); Tribe, *American Constitutional Law*, §15–13, p. 943. Four members of the Supreme Court itself have also apparently taken this view. See Carey v. Population Services International, 431 U.S. 678, 694 n. 17 (Brennan, J., concurring in the result) ["We observe that the Court has not definitively answered the difficult question whether and to what extent the Constitution prohibits state statutes regulating [private consensual sexual] behavior among adults."]
19. *Supra* note 15.
20. People v. Onofre, *supra* note 18 at 953.
21. Md. ANN. CODE §27–554.
22. See Pryor v. Municipal Court, 25 Cal. 2d 238, 158 Cal. Rptr. 330, 599 P.2d 636 (1979); Pederson v. Richmond, 219 Va. 1061, 254 S.E. 2d 95 (1979); State v. Tusek, 52 Or. App. 997, 630 P.2d 892 (1981). See also People v. Gibson, 184 Colo. 444, 521 P.2d 774 (1974); State v. Phipps, 58 Ohio St. 2d 271, 389 N.E. 2d 1128 (1979); Commonwealth v. Sefranka, 414 N.E. 2d 602 (Mass. 1980).
23. See, e.g. People v. Berck, 32 N.Y. 2d 567, 347 N.Y.S. 2d 33, 300 N.E. 2d 411 (1973).
24. N.Y. PENAL LAW §240.35(3). At this writing, the New York statute is under constitutional challenge in the state courts on the basis of People v. Onofre, *supra* note 15. See People v. Uplinger, Misc. 2d 403,444 N.&.S. 2d 373 (Buffalo City Ct. 1981), *aff'd* 449 N.Y.S. 2d 916 (Erie County Ct. 1982), *appeal docheted*.
25. See e.g. *Matter of Kimball*, 33 N.Y. 2d 586, 347 N.Y.S. 2d 453 (1973).
26. See Morrison v. State Board of Education, 1 Cal. 3d 214, 461 P.2d 375, 82 Cal. Rptr. 175 (1969). See also Burton v. Cascade School District, 512 F.2d 850 (9th Cir.), *cert denied*, 423 U.S. 839 (1975). But see Gaylord v. Tacoma School District, No. 10, *supra* note 2, *cert. denied*, 434 U.S. 879 (1977).

X

The Rights of *Transvestites* and *Transsexuals*

Although transvestites and transsexuals are often not homosexual in orientation, it's appropriate that a chapter on
their problems be included in a book on gay rights, since the
legal and factual issues are closely related.

What do the terms transsexual and transvestite mean?

Gender identity is the awareness of oneself as a male or
female. It is a basic component of personality that is extremely difficult to change. The transsexual's gender identity
is not the same as his or her actual physical anatomy, and
dressing in clothes of the opposite sex and appearing to the
world as a member of the opposite sex, are essential parts of
the transsexual's gender identity.[1]

Transvestites, who are usually male, wear some or all the
clothing of the opposite sex for occasional personal gratification, but not out of a psychological identification with the sex.

Although psychiatrists and psychologists persist in the attempt, they have been generally unsuccessful in "curing"
transvestites and transsexuals.[2] The patients do not wish to be
"cured" in the sense of reversing their gender identity, or
changing their personal habits, but they often seek psychiatric help because society will not accept them for what they
are. Transsexuals have, however, been helped by sex-reassignment surgery and hormone therapy, which harmonizes anatomical sex, with psychological gender identification.

The medical term for transsexualism is *gender dysphoria*.

May transsexuals and transvestites be arrested for cross-dressing in public?

Yes. Anti-cross-dressing ordinances exist in many cities,[3] and according to one survey taken in 1971, under state laws in Arizona, California, Colorado, Idaho, Nevada, Oklahoma, Oregon, Texas, Utah, and Washington, cross-dressing is a criminal act.[4] In many jurisdictions, impersonating, or masquerading as, a member of the opposite sex is illegal on the basis of vagrancy or disorderly conduct laws. For example, in New York, a person may be guilty of loitering if he or she, "[b]eing masked or in any manner disguised by unusual or unnatural attire or facial alteration, loiters, remains or congregates in a public place with other persons so masked or disguised. . . ."[5]

As explained below, there are serious questions about the constitutionality of these statutes. But to protect yourself, you should check the current status of the law in your vicinity.

How did cross-dressing laws originate?

Wearing the clothing of the opposite sex was forbidden by the Jewish religion as part of an early code of sexual morality.[6] Joan of Arc was considered a heretic partly because she dressed as a man in violation of spiritual law.[7] According to New York's former cross-dressing statute, individuals were not able to wear disguises, or have painted faces in public.[8] That statute was adopted in the nineteenth century in response to the actions of farmers who, during anti-rent riots, murdered law-enforcement officers while disguised as Indians, or while wearing dresses.[9]

The legislative purpose of such statutes is usually said to be to prevent the efforts of criminals to avoid recognition, or to perpetrate frauds.

Are cross-dressing laws constitutional?

The highest courts of two states have called into question the constitutionality of cross-dressing statutes. In 1975, the Supreme Court of Ohio struck down a Columbus ordinance prohibiting a person from wearing in public "a dress not belonging to his or her sex," on the ground that it was so vague that it violated the constitutional guarantee of due process of law. The court noted that "[a]t the present time, clothing is sold for both sexes which is so similar in appear-

ance that 'a person of ordinary intelligence' might not be able
to identify it as male or female dress," and also that "it is not
uncommon today for individuals to purposely, but innocent-
ly, wear apparel which is intended for wear by those of the
opposite sex." Therefore, said the court, the average person
simply could not tell by the mere phrase "dress not belonging
to his or her sex," what was prohibited, and what was not.[10]

Three years later, the Supreme Court of Illinois reversed
two convictions in Chicago under a similar ordinance, but for
a different reason. The defendants in question, both male,
had testified at their trial that they were transsexuals who
were wearing female clothing at the time of their arrest as
part of psychiatric therapy in preparation for sex-reassignment
operations. The court noted that the Illinois legislature had
"implicitly recognized the necessity and validity of such surgery" by recently enacting a statute authorizing the issuance
of a new birth certificate after a sex-reassignment operation,
and declared that "[i]t would be inconsistent to permit sex-
reassignment surgery yet, at the same time, impede the
necessary therapy in preparation for such surgery." It then
proceeded to balance the defendants' right to choose such
surgery against the "aesthetic preference" of society against
cross-dressing, and concluded that the convictions could not
stand. Applying the ordinance to those defendants under
those circumstances, said the court, amounted to an "unconstitutional infringement of their liberty interest."[11]

It is important to note that the Illinois court did not invali-
date the ordinance, but merely ruled it inapplicable under
the Constitution to those two defendants. Nevertheless, the
court's opinion, which is filled with references to each individual's right to choose (within limits) his or her own appearance and life-style, suggests that such ordinances are in fact
unconstitutional by their very nature.

As these two opinions indicate, different arguments can be
made for the unconstitutionality of cross-dressing statutes.
First, they can be viewed as impermissibly vague, as in the
Ohio case.[12] Secondly, they can be seen as an unconstitutional intrusion on the individual's right to privacy, as in the
Illinois case. (The U.S. Supreme Court has made it clear that
the right to privacy includes the right to personal autonomy—
the freedom to make certain individual decisions without
unwarranted governmental interference.[13])

Thirdly, cross-dressing statutes may be said to infringe on the individual's right to free expression under the First Amendment, since one's choice of clothing is indicative of one's beliefs, concerns, and life-style. Indeed, the U.S. Supreme Court has already explicitly recognized the symbolic power of certain styles of dress or articles of clothing, at least in certain circumstances.[14]

Fourthly, such statutes may be unconstitutional because they punish a defendant for what he is, rather than for what he does. Many transvestites and transsexuals apparently feel compelled to wear clothing of the opposite sex. Cross-dressing statutes make a criminal act from what may be involuntary behavior. In *Robinson* v. *California,* the U.S. Supreme Court held that a state could not punish a defendant merely because he was a narcotics addict.[15] The clear implication of *Robinson* is that any statute that inflicts punishment on the basis of one's status, as cross-dressing statutes arguably do, violates the constitutional prohibition against cruel and unusual punishment.

What may transvestites and transsexuals do to protect themselves from arrest and conviction?

Some transsexuals have successfully resisted convictions under cross-dressing laws on nonconstitutional grounds. For example, a Columbus, Ohio, male transsexual was arrested for appearing in public in feminine dress, but the court dismissed the case because the defendant had "an irresistible impulse" to dress in the clothing of the opposite sex. The court drew an analogy to the criminal defense of insanity.[16] In Texas, a transvestite avoided conviction on the ground that a state statute outlawing wearing a disguise in public was inapplicable to him because, although he was dressed in female clothing, his identity was known to the arresting officer.[17]

Precautionary measures may be taken to avoid arrest. Transsexuals who desire sex-reassignment surgery are often required to live in the proposed sex role for as much as one year before the operation will be performed. Such a person should carry a card or letter from a doctor stating that crossdressing is required for medical treatment. State and county health departments may provide official letters of confirmation to transsexuals who present an affidavit from a physician.[18] The cards or letters do not guarantee that transsexuals will not be prosecuted for cross-dressing, but they will help to establish that such behavior is not done to defraud, or to cause disorder.

If a transsexual is imprisoned for cross-dressing or for some other crime, may he or she be incarcerated with prisoners of the opposite psychological sex?

Yes. As for preoperative transsexuals, the usual inclination of prison officials is to group anatomical males with males and anatomical females with females despite the possibility that psychological trauma or physical danger may be created for the transsexual. In at least one instance, the authorities have even incarcerated a *post*operative female transsexual with male prisoners.[19] It has been reported, however, that the Men's House of Detention in New York City separates transvestites and transsexuals from the general prison population for their protection.[20]

While no court has yet decided the issue of the constitutionality of the practice of refusing to incarcerate transsexuals with members of the sex with which they identify, at least two have shown some sympathy for transsexuals facing imprisonment. An appellate court in Illinois in 1972 reduced the sentence of a preoperative transsexual to probation because the defendant would have had difficulty adjusting to the masculine environment of prison, and incarceration would not have encouraged rehabilitation.[21] (A psychiatrist had testified regarding the harmful consequences of sending the prisoner to an all-male prison.) More recently, a court in New York awarded a defendant money damages as compensation for the harassment she had received while in police custody, including being booked under her previous male name, even though she had already had sex-reassignment surgery.[22]

Is sex-reassignment surgery for transsexuals legal in the United States?

Yes. Although surgery designed to coordinate a person's physical anatomy with his or her psychological gender identity is not universally accepted by the medical profession,[23] it is not illegal. Physicians formerly pointed to the "mayhem" statutes, which outlaw maiming or disfiguring the body, as a reason for not performing sex-conversion surgery. The mayhem laws originated in England, and were intended to prevent men from dismembering themselves or others, in order to avoid military service.[24] Those laws arguably are not applicable to medical sex conversion, however, since the crime requires a specific intent to maim, and surgery designed to benefit the patient psychologically, may be said not to have such an intent.[25] In any event, such surgery is not performed with frequency. The first gender-identity clinic performing sex-reassignment surgery was established at Johns Hopkins Hospital in Baltimore in 1966.[26] By June 1973, there were eighteen clinics or private surgeons in the United States performing the operation.[27]

Physicians who perform sex-reassignment surgery commonly require the transsexual to be screened by psychiatrists, undergo hormone treatment, and live as a member of the desired sex for up to one year. Given the fundamental and irreversible nature of the surgical transformation, such screening procedures are wise to assure that the individual has considered the decision to undergo the operation with sufficient care.

Will health insurance or the government pay for sex-reassignment surgery?

Blue Cross has, in some instances, paid for at least part of the costs of such surgery. However, since policies differ, it is important to examine your policy carefully, and then to make inquiries to determine the exact scope of coverage.[28]

Every state, except Arizona, has a medical-assistance program for needy persons. Those programs will pay for surgery, however, only if it is "medically necessary." Thus, operations that are purely cosmetic are excluded.[29] In 1972, Medicaid authorities in New York turned down an application for sex-reassignment surgery on this basis, relying on the testimony of one psychiatrist to the effect that the applicant's condition caused him "no disturbance in thinking or suicidal inclination," and the New York Court of Appeals, the highest court in the state, later refused to overturn that determination.[30] Several other courts have struck down regulations or policies explicitly prohibiting the funding of *all* sex-reassignment operations, recognizing that at least in some cases, such surgery might be shown to meet the standard of medical necessity.[31] Furthermore, an appellate court in California recently ordered that state's Department of Health to grant an application for sex-reassignment surgery, stating, "[I]t is clearly impossible to conclude that transsexual surgery is cosmetic surgery."[32] And even in New York, one court has recognized that in some instances, there might be a "medical necessity" for the operation.[33]

As for the federal government's Medicare program, which covers primarily the elderly, the current policy is apparently to deny funds for sex-reassignment surgery, in part because of doubts about the "medical efficacy" of the procedure.[34]

Once sex-reassignment surgery is completed, does the transsexual have the right to full legal recognition of his or her new identity?

Dr. Harry Benjamin, an expert on transsexualism, has stated:

> After [sex-reassignment surgery] has been done and we are dealing with a *fait accompli*, it should be made as easy as possible for the patient to succeed in his or her new life. And the legal recognition of this new life is a very essential part indeed.[35]

Achieving legal recognition of the postoperative sex is, however, often quite difficult.

The sex designation on one's birth certificate is the key to the legal establishment of sex for most purposes—obtaining marriage licenses, passports, and insurance policies. At least three states—Arizona, Illinois, and Louisiana—have statutes that provide that postoperative transsexuals be issued new birth certificates.[36] Other states permit a change of sex designation by administrative regulation or practice.[37]

Many jurisdictions are less enlightened. For example, the New York City Department of Health has repeatedly refused to change sex designations on birth certificates, and the courts have so far declined to overrule the department. The issue first arose in 1965, when, in response to several applications for such changes on birth certificates, the department asked its Board of Health for a policy determination, and the board called upon the New York Academy of Medicine to study the matter and submit its recommendations. The academy issued a report that contained the following conclusions:

1. Male-to-female transsexuals are still chromosomally males while ostensibly females;

2. It is questionable whether laws and records such as the birth certificate should be changed and thereby used as a means to help psychologically ill persons in their social adaptation.

The Committee is therefore opposed to a change of sex on birth certificates in transsexualism.

. . . The desire of concealment of a change of sex by the transsexual is outweighed by the public interest for protection against fraud.[38]

Shortly thereafter, the board passed a resolution adopting those conclusions. The new policy was challenged in state court, but the court concluded that it lacked the authority to overturn it because it was not clearly "arbitrary."[39]

The city has since modified its policy somewhat. Its current practice is apparently to issue a new birth certificate acknowledging the new name, but deleting any reference to sex.[40] This can hardly be called a satisfactory solution. The omission of a sexual identity denies transsexuals the legal recognition of their new sex, which many doctors believe to be necessary for satisfactory postoperative adjustment. Additionally, the lack of sex designation may present an obstacle for a postoperative transsexual who wishes to marry.

Not all government agencies require proof of a new or amended birth certificate, however, to change the sex designation on an official document. Some, including the Social Security Administration, require no more than completion of a simple form to correct or amend their records. Others may agree to make the desired changes merely upon receipt of a letter from a physician stating that a sex-reassignment operation has been performed.[41]

As for changes of name, traditionally a person may adopt any first name he or she prefers, as long as there is no intent to defraud.[42] In most jurisdictions, a court order is not even necessary to establish a new name. The new name may become one's lawful designation merely through constant and exclusive use. But a change of name does not by itself legally change a person's sex.

May a transsexual marry as a member of his or her chosen sex?

A marriage between a preoperative transsexual and another person of the same anatomical sex is generally viewed as homosexual, and therefore void.[43] (As explained in chapter VIII, there is at present no state that recognizes the validity of homosexual marriages.)

The law is slightly more favorable for postoperative transsexuals. Although there is precedent to the effect that a chromosomal male is always a male and is therefore not entitled to marry as a female even when surgery has altered his anatomy,[44] many postoperative transsexuals have in fact married, and at least one court has recognized such marriages as valid.[45] A transsexual who does not reveal the fact of sex reassignment to the prospective spouse may, however, run the risk of having the marriage annulled on grounds of fraud.[46]

With respect to marriages entered into in the preoperative sex role, many clinics recommend that a divorce be obtained prior to sex-reassignment surgery.[47] In a New Jersey case, a wife was granted a divorce on the grounds of "extreme cruelty" because her husband's "dress, manner, occupational interests and associations [were] all designed to enhance his feeling of being a woman."[48] Some transsexuals continue to live with their spouses after surgery as "sisters" or "brothers."[49]

May employers discriminate against persons who are transsexuals or transvestites?

Unless the locality in question has legislation specifically outlawing discrimination on the basis of affectional or sexual preference (and even then it may not be clear that the phrase covers transsexuals and transvestites), there is probably nothing to prohibit an employer from firing or refusing to hire or promote a transsexual or transvestite. For example, the Civil Rights Act of 1964 prohibiting discrimination on the basis of sex by most employers has been interpreted not to cover transsexuals.[50]

The situation is slightly more encouraging for transvestites and transsexuals who work for the government, whether on the federal, state, or local level. The equal protection and Due Process Clauses of the U.S. Constitution require the government, at a minimum, to act rationally in its treatment of employees. Therefore, a governmental employer must demonstrate a rational basis for any attempt to treat a transvestite or transsexual differently from other employees. It is unclear at this point what might constitute such a rational basis for discrimination—whether, for example, the alleged discomfort or embarrassment of fellow coworkers might be enough.

One of the most highly publicized cases involving employment discrimination against a transsexual is *In Re Grossman*. In that case, a school board in New Jersey suspended without pay, a fifty-two-year-old male tenured elementary music teacher after he had undergone sex-reassignment surgery. After the matter was brought before the state's commissioner of education, the commissioner ordered the teacher's dismissal because of the alleged "potential her presence in the classroom presents for psychological harm to the students" of the township. A New Jersey appellate court upheld the dismissal, even though it acknowledged that Mrs. Grossman's proficiency as a teacher was not in question, ruling that it was "reasonably probable" that her students would suffer emotional harm if she were retained.[51] However, the same court later determined that Mrs. Grossman was entitled to a monthly pension from the statewide Teachers' Pension and Annuity Fund because of her inability to obtain a teaching position.[52]

May transvestites or transsexuals be denied custody of their children, or visitation rights?

Possibly, depending upon a particular court's view of what is in the best interest of the children. Courts are generally given wide discretion.[53]

In a 1973 Colorado case, a female-to-male transsexual, the mother of four daughters, was permitted to retain custody of her children in a legal challenge from her former husband, despite the fact that she had even gone so far as to marry a woman.[54]

Where can I go to obtain more information or assistance?

The Gender Identity Clinic of the University of Texas Medical Branch at Galveston, operates an information center on transsexualism. The address is Janus Information Facility, The University of Texas Medical Branch, 415 Texas Avenue, Galveston, TX 77550. An organization called Confide Personal

Counseling Services, Inc., Box 56, Tappan, NY 10983, also provides information and counseling for transsexuals and transvestites and publishes a newspaper entitled *Transition*.

NOTES

1. See generally Green and Money, eds., *Transsexualism and Sex Reassignment* (1969).
2. See generally Stoller, *Sex and Gender* (1968); Holloway, *Transsexuals— Their Legal Sex*, 40 U. Colo. L. Rev. 282, 283 (1968). Dr. Richard Green recommends behavior-modification therapy for children with atypical sexual identities in order to avoid the social problems which face the transsexual adult. Green, *Sexual Identity Conflict in Children and Adults*, 245 (1974).
3. See, e.g. Section 192–8 of the Municipal Code of the City of Chicago, which states:
    > Any person who shall appear in a public place . . . in a dress not belonging to his or her sex, with intent to conceal his or her sex, . . . shall be fined not less than twenty dollars nor more than five hundred dollars for each offense.

    Section 192-8 was declared unconstitutional as applied to two male transsexuals by the Supreme Court of Illinois in Chicago v. Wilson, *infra* n. 11.
4. Erickson Educational Foundation, "Legal Aspects of Transsexualism," 3 (1971).
5. N.Y. PENAL LAW §240.35(4).
6. Comment, *Transsexualism, Sex Reassignment Surgery and the Law*, 56 Cornell L. Rev. 963, 964 (1971).
7. *Id.*
8. Former §887(7) of N.Y. Penal Law.
9. See People v. Archibald, 58 Misc. 2d 862, 864, 296 N.Y.S. 2d 834, 837 (Sup. Ct. 1968) *(dissenting opinion)*.
10. Columbus v. Rogers, 41 Ohio St. 2d 161, 324 N.E. 2d 563 (1975).
11. Chicago v. Wilson, 75 Ill. 2d 525, 389 N.E. 2d 522 (1978). See also Doe v. McConn, 489 F. Supp. 76 (S.D. Tex. 1980), striking down as unconstitutional, Houston's cross-dressing ordinance.
12. See also Cincinnati v. Adams, 330 N.E. 2d 463 (Municipal Ct. Ohio 1974).
13. See, e.g. Roe v. Wade, 410 U.S. 113 (1973), and Eisenstadt v. Baird, 405 U.S. 438, 453–54 (1972).
14. See Tinker v. Des Moines Independent Community School District, 393 U.S. 503 (1969); Kelley v. Johnson, 425 U.S. 249 (1976) (Marshall, J., dissenting). See generally Craft and Hodel, *City of Chicago v. Wilson and Constitutional Protection for Personal Appearance, Cross-Dressing as an Element of Sexual Identity*, 30 Hastings L. J. 1151 (1979).

15. 370 U.S. 660 (1962).

16. Columbus v. Zanders, 25 Ohio Misc. 144, 266 N.E. 2d 602 (1970).

17. Garcia v. State, 443 S.W. 2d 847 (Tex. Crim. App. 1969).

18. *Supra* note 4, at 3.

19. Grant v. Doyle, 76 Civ. 3813 (S.D.N.Y. Dec. 20, 1978) (unreported mem. decision).

20. *New York Times* Magazine, Feb. 17, 1974, 19.

21. People v. Steadman, 3 Ill. App. 3d 1045, 280 N.E. 2d 17 (1972).

22. Grant v. Doyle, *supra* note 19.

23. Holloway, *supra* note 2, at 286. See also *New York Times*, Oct. 2, 1979, Cl.

24. Comment, *supra* note 6, at 987.

25. *Id*. See Holloway, *supra* note 2, at 284.

26. Holloway, *supra* note 2, at 284. Johns Hopkins has since stopped performing sex-reassignment surgery. See *New York Times, supra* note 23.

27. Letter from Erickson Educational Foundation, June 1973.

28. In Davidson v. Aetna Life & Casualty Insurance Co., 101 Misc. 2d 1, 420 N.Y.S. 2d 450 (Sup. Ct. 1979), the employer's private insurance carrier was ordered to pay for an employee's sex-reassignment operation because the employee had proven that the surgery was "feasible and required for [his] health and well being."

29. E.g. N.Y. SOCIAL SERVICES LAW §365–a provides that medical assistance means "care, services and supplies which are necessary to prevent, diagnose, correct or cure conditions in the person that cause acute suffering, endanger life, result in illness or infirmity, interfere with his capacity for normal activity, or threaten some significant handicap."

30. Denise R. v. Lavine, 39 N.Y. 2d 279, 383 N.Y.S. 2d 568, 347 N.E. 2d 893 (1976).

31. See Pinneke v. Preisser, 623 F.2d 546 (8th Cir. 1980); Doe v. Department of Public Welfare, 257 N.W. 2d 816 (Minn. 1977). But see Rush v. Parham, 440 F. Supp. 383 (N.D. Ga. 1977), rev'd, 625 F.2d 1150 (5th Cir. 1980).

32. G.B. v. Lackner, 80 Cal. App. 3d 64; 145 Cal. Rptr. 555 (1978).

33. Vickers v. Toia, 66 A.D. 2d 747, 411 N.Y.S. 2d 599 (1978).

34. Letter to Thomas B. Stoddard from Jacqualine G. Wilson, Regional Medicare Director for the Department of Health, Education and Welfare, Region II, dated Feb. 11, 1980.

35. Quoted in Comment, *supra* note 6, at 971.

36. ARIZ. REV. STAT. ANN. §36–326; ILL. ANN. STAT. Ch. 111 ½ §73/17; LA. REV. STAT. ANN. §40:336.

37. See Walz, *Transsexuals and the Law*, 5 J. Cont. L. 181, 192, n. 67 (1979).

38. Quoted in Anonymous v. Weiner, 50 Misc. 2d 380, 382–83, 270 N.Y.S. 2d 319, 322 (Sup. Ct. 1966).

39. Anonymous v. Weiner, 50 Misc. 2d at 384–85, 270 N.Y.S. 2d at 323–24. For another instance in which a court concluded that it lacked the authority to order a change of sex on a birth certificate, see K. v. Health Division, 277 Ore. 371, 560 P.2d 1070 (1977). But see In re Anonymous, 57 Misc. 2d 813, 293 N.Y.S. 2d 834 (Civ. Ct. 1968).

40. See Hartin v. Director of Bureau of Records and Statistics, 75 Misc. 2d 229, 347 N.Y.S. 2d 515 (Sup. Ct. 1973); Anonymous v. Mellon, 91 Misc. 2d 375, 398 N.Y.S. 2d 99 (Sup. Ct. 1977).

41. See Clark, *Legal Aspects of Transsexualism,* published for the Janus Information Facility of the University of Texas Medical Branch at Galveston, F–1 to F–6 (1978).

42. See, e.g. In re Anonymous, 64 Misc. 2d 309, 314 N.Y.S. 2d 668 (Civ. Ct. 1970).

43. See e.g. Anonymous v. Anonymous, 67 Misc. 2d 982, 325 N.Y.S. 2d 499 (Sup. Ct. 1971); Frances B. v. Mark B., 78 Misc. 2d 112, 355 N.Y.S. 2d 712 (Sup. Ct. 1974).

44. Corbett v. Corbett, 2 All E.R. 33 (1970) (Great Britain).

45. M.T. v. J.T., 140 N.J. Super, 77, 355 A.2d 204 (App. Div. 1976).

46. Cf. Frances B. v. Mark B., *supra* note 43.

47. *Supra* note 4, at 10.

48. L.P. v. S.P., 121 N.J. Super. 368, 297 A.2d 202 (1972).

49. See *New York Times,* Oct. 23, 1973, 42.

50. See Voyles v. Ralph K. Davies Medical Center, 403 F. Supp. 456 (N.D. Cal. 1975), *aff'd,* 570 F.2d 354 (9th Cir. 1978); Powell v. Read's Inc., 436 F. Supp. 369 (D. Md. 1977); Holloway v. Arthur Anderson and Co., 566 F.2d 659 (9th Cir. 1977); Summers v. Budget Marketing, Inc., 667 F.2d 748 (8th Cir. 1982). Cf. Kirkpatrick v. Seligman and Latz, Inc., 475 F. Supp. 145 (M.D. Fla. 1979), *aff'd,* 636 F.2d 1047 (5th Cir. 1981) (holding that transsexuals are not a "suspect class" for purposes of equal protection analysis).

51. 127 N.J. Super. 13, 316 A.2d 39 (App. Div. 1974).

52. 157 N.J. Super. 165, 384 A.2d 855 (App. Div. 1978).

53. See chapter VIII.

54. Christian v. Randall, 33 Colo. App. 129, 516 P.2d 132 (1973).

Appendix A

Criminal Statutes Relating to Consensual Homosexual Acts Between Adults*

ALABAMA

STATUTE: Definition of Deviate Sexual Intercourse
           13A–6–60

OFFENSE: Any sex act between persons not married in-
           volving the sex organs of one person, and the
           mouth or anus of another.

STATUS: n/a†

PENALTY: n/a

STATUTE: Sexual Misconduct
           13A–6–65

OFFENSE: Engaging in deviate sexual intercourse. Consent
           is no defense.

*This table sets forth, by state, all those criminal statues in the United
States that relate specifically to consensual homosexual acts between
adults, with one major exception: sexual acts, or the solicitation of sexual
acts, for money, which are still illegal in virtually every jurisdiction.

All statutory citations refer to the criminal code of the particular state.
In some states and for some crimes, higher penalties accrue upon subsequent convictions.

The authors gratefully acknowledge the assistance of Mary Shannon,
a student at New York University School of Law, in the preparation of
this table.

†not applicable

STATUS: Class A misd.††
PENALTY: NTE** 1 yr. a/o*** $2,000

STATUTE: Indecent Exposure
             13A–6–68
OFFENSE: Purposeful exposure of one's genitals in a public
             place or on the private premises of another
             person, under circumstances likely to cause af-
             front or alarm.
STATUS: Class A misd.
PENALTY: NTE 1 yr. a/o $2,000

STATUTE: Loitering
             13A–11–9
OFFENSE: Remaining or wandering in a public place for
             the purpose of engaging, or soliciting another
             person to engage, in deviate sexual intercourse.
STATUS: Violation
PENALTY: NTE 30 days a/o $200

STATUTE: Registration of Sex Offenders
             13A–11–200
OFFENSE: Individual convicted of sexual misconduct or
             indecent exposure must register with the county
             sheriff.
STATUS: Felony
PENALTY: NLT††† 1 yr., NTE 5 yrs. a/o $1,000

STATUTE: Public Lewdness
             13A–12–130
OFFENSE: Exposure of anus or genitals in public place.
STATUS: Class C misd.
PENALTY: NTE 3 mos. a/o $500

**Not to exceed
***and/or
††misdemeanor
†††Not less than

ALASKA[1]

STATUTE: Disorderly Conduct
11.61.110

OFFENSE: Intentional exposure of genitals, buttocks, anus, or female breast to another person, having an offensive or insulting effect.

STATUS: Class B misd.

PENALTY: Discretionary sentencing involving a combination of community work, fine NTE $1,000, a/o imprisonment NTE 10 days.

ARIZONA

STATUTE: Indecent Exposure
13–1402

OFFENSE: Exposure of genitals, anus, or female breast to another person, having an offensive or alarming effect.

STATUS: Class 3 misd.

PENALTY: NTE 30 days a/o $500

STATUTE: Public Sexual Indecency
13–1403

OFFENSE: Direct or indirect fondling of any part of the genitals, anus, or female breast, or oral contact with another person's sex organs, or sexual intercourse with another in the presence of another person, having an offensive or alarming effect.

STATUS: Class 2 misd.

PENALTY: NTE 4 mos. a/o $750

STATUTE: Crime Against Nature
13–1411

OFFENSE: Anal or oral intercourse.

STATUS: Class 3 misd.

PENALTY: NTE 30 days a/o $500

STATUTE: Lewd & Lascivious Acts
13–1412

[1]Decriminalized private consensual adult homosexual acts, 1978 ASL §21 ch. 166 (eff. Jan. 1, 1980).

OFFENSE: Commission of any lewd or lascivious act with another in an unnatural manner.
STATUS: Class 3 misd.
PENALTY: NTE 30 days a/o $500

STATUTE: Loitering
13–2905
OFFENSE: Remaining in public place and soliciting another person in an offensive or disturbing manner to engage in any sexual offense.
STATUS: Class 3 misd.
PENALTY: NTE 30 days a/o $500

ARKANSAS

STATUTE: Public Sexual Indecency
41–1811
OFFENSE: Engaging in sexual intercourse, any sex act involving the mouth or anus of one person, and the penis of another, or any act of sexual contact in a public place.
STATUS: Class A misd.
PENALTY: NTE 1 yr. a/o $1,000

STATUTE: Indecent Exposure
41–1812
OFFENSE: Exposure of one's sex organs in a public place.
STATUS: Class A misd.
PENALTY: NTE 1 yr. a/o $1,000

STATUTE: Sodomy
41–1813
OFFENSE: Performing any act of sexual gratification involving oral or anal penetration by the penis of a person of the same sex, or vaginal or anal penetration by any body member of a person of the same sex.
STATUS: Class A misd.
PENALTY: NTE 1 yr. a/o $1,000

STATUTE: Loitering
41–2914

OFFENSE: Lingering or remaining in a public place for the purpose of engaging or soliciting someone to engage in deviate sexual activity.

STATUS: Class C misd.

PENALTY: NTE 30 days a/o $100

CALIFORNIA[2]

STATUTE: Registration of Sex Offenders
290

OFFENSE: Individual convicted of disorderly conduct must register with local chief of police.

STATUS: Misd.

PENALTY: NTE 6 mos. a/o $500

STATUTE: Lewd or Obscene Conduct
314

OFFENSE: Willful exposure of one's genitals in any public place or where others are present who are likely to be annoyed.

STATUS: Misd.

PENALTY: NTE 6 mos. a/o $500

STATUTE: Disorderly Conduct
647

OFFENSE: Soliciting or engaging in lewd or dissolute conduct in a public place, or loitering about in a public toilet for the purpose of soliciting or engaging in any lewd or lascivious act.[3]

STATUS: Misd.

PENALTY: NTE 6 mos. a/o $500

STATUTE: Outraging Public Decency
650–½

[2]Decriminalized private consensual adult homosexual acts, 1975 Cal. Stat., ch. 71 §7 (eff. July 1, 1976).

[3]Interpreted to cover only public conduct involving touching of the genitals, buttocks or female breast for purposes of sexual arousal, gratification, annoyance, or offense. Pryor v. Municipal Court, 25 Cal. 3d 238, 158 Cal. Rptr. 330, 599 P.2d 636 (1979).

OFFENSE: Commission of an act which openly outrages public decency (no further statutory explanation given).

STATUS: Misd.

PENALTY: NTE 6 mos. a/o $500

COLORADO[4]

STATUTE: Public Indecency
            18–7–301

OFFENSE: Performance of oral or anal sex, lewd exposure of one's body for sexual arousal, or lewd fondling of another person in a public place.

STATUS: Class 1 petty offense

PENALTY: NTE 6 mos. a/o $500

STATUTE: Indecent Exposure
            18–7–302

OFFENSE: Exposure of one's genitals to any person under circumstances likely to cause affront or alarm.

STATUS: Class 2 misd.

PENALTY: NLT 3 mos., NTE 1 yr. a/o NLT $250, NTE $1,000

STATUTE: Disorderly Conduct
            18–9–106

OFFENSE: Coarse and obviously offensive utterance, gesture, or display in public that tends to incite an immediate breach of the peace.

STATUS: Class 1 petty offense

PENALTY: NTE 6 mos. a/o $500

STATUTE: Loitering
            18–9–112

OFFENSE: Lingering, remaining, or wandering in a public place for the purpose of engaging in, or soliciting, any deviate sexual intercourse.[5]

[4]Decriminalized private consensual adult homosexual acts, 1971 Colo. Sess. Laws, ch. 121, §1 (eff. Jan. 1, 1972).
[5]Held unconstitutional. People v. Gibson, 184 Colo. 444, 521 P.2d 774 (1974).

STATUS: Class 1 petty offense
PENALTY: NTE 6 mos. a/o $500

CONNECTICUT[6]

STATUTE: Breach of Peace
53A–181
OFFENSE: Using abusive or obscene language or gestures in a public place intending to cause inconvenience, annoyance, or alarm.
STATUS: Class B misd.
PENALTY: NTE 6 mos. a/o $1,000

STATUTE: Public Indecency
53A–186
OFFENSE: Performance of anal or oral sex, lewd exposure of one's body for sexual arousal, or lewd fondling or caressing of another's body in a public place.
STATUS: Class B misd.
PENALTY: NTE 6 mos. a/o $1,000

DELAWARE[7]

STATUTE: Indecent Exposure
11–768
OFFENSE: Exposure of genitals to another person under circumstances likely to cause affront or alarm.
STATUS: Class B misd.
PENALTY: NTE 6 mos. a/o $500

STATUTE: Disorderly Conduct
11–1301
OFFENSE: Public display of offensive utterance or gesture intending to cause inconvenience, annoyance, or alarm.
STATUS: Class B misd.
PENALTY: NTE 6 mos. a/o $500

---

[6]Decriminalized private consensual adult homosexual acts, 1969 Public Act 828,§214 (eff. Nov. 1, 1971).
[7]Decriminalized private consensual adult homosexual acts, 58 Del. Laws, ch. 497,§1 (eff. Apr. 1, 1973).

STATUTE: Loitering
11–1321

OFFENSE: Remaining in a public place for the purpose of engaging or soliciting another person to engage in sexual intercourse or deviate sexual intercourse.

STATUS: Violation

PENALTY: Discretionary fine

STATUTE: Lewdness
11–1341

OFFENSE: Performance of lewd act in public place. (No further statutory explanation given.)

STATUS: Class B misd.

PENALTY: NTE 6 mos. a/o $500

DISTRICT OF COLUMBIA

STATUTE: Profane & Indecent Language
22–1107

OFFENSE: Making rude or obscene gestures or comments to others in a public place.[8]

STATUS: Misd.

PENALTY: NTE 90 a/o $250

STATUTE: Lewdness
22–1112

OFFENSE: Exposing one's body in an obscene or indecent manner, making a lewd, obscene, or indecent sexual proposal, or committing a lewd, obscene, or indecent act. (No further statutory explanation given.)

STATUS: Misd.

PENALTY: NTE 90 days a/o $300

STATUTE: Inviting for Purposes of Prostitution
22–2701

OFFENSE: Inviting, enticing, persuading, or addressing another for any immoral or lewd purpose. (No further statutory explanation given).

---

[8]Construed to be limited to conduct creating a substantial risk of provoking violence, or conduct so grossly offensive as to constitute a nuisance. In re M.W.G., 427 A.2d 440 (1981).

STATUS: Misd.
PENALTY: NTE 90 days a/o $300

STATUTE: Sodomy
22–3502
OFFENSE: Performing any sex act involving the mouth or anus of one person, and the sex organs of another.
STATUS: Felony
PENALTY: NTE 10 yrs a/o $1,000

FLORIDA

STATUTE: Prostitution
796.07
OFFENSE: Engaging in sexual intercourse for hire, or licentious sexual intercourse without hire, or in any indecent or obscene act.
STATUS: Misd. second degree
PENALTY: NTE 60 days a/o $500

STATUTE: Lewd & Lascivious Behavior
798.02
OFFENSE: Open and gross lewdness and lascivious behavior. (No further statutory explanation given.)
STATUS: Misd. second degree
PENALTY: NTE 60 days a/o $500

STATUTE: Unnatural & Lascivious Act
§800.02
OFFENSE: Commission of any historically forbidden sex act; that is, sodomy, fellatio, or cunnilingus.
STATUS: Misd. second degree
PENALTY: NTE 60 days a/o $500

STATUTE: Exposure of Sexual Organs
800.03
OFFENSE: Exposure of one's sex organs in any public place except in a place specifically set apart for that purpose.
STATUS: Misd. first degree
PENALTY: NTE 1 yr. a/o $1,000

GEORGIA

STATUTE:	Sodomy 26–2002
OFFENSE:	Any sex act involving the mouth or anus of one person, and the sex organs of another.
STATUS:	Felony
PENALTY:	NLT 1 yr. NTE 20 yrs.

STATUTE:	Solicitation of Sodomy 26–2003
OFFENSE:	Soliciting any person to perform or submit to an act of sodomy.
STATUS:	Misd.
PENALTY:	NTE 1 yr. a/o $1,000

STATUTE:	Public Indecency 26–2011
OFFENSE:	Performing sexual intercourse lewdly, exposing one's sex organs, lewdly appearing in a state of partial or complete nudity, or lewdly caressing the body of another person in a public place.
STATUS:	Misd.
PENALTY:	NTE 1 yr. a/o $1,000

HAWAII[9]

STATUTE:	Indecent Exposure 707–738
OFFENSE:	Exposure of one's genitals to another person under circumstances likely to cause affront or alarm.
STATUS:	Petty misd.
PENALTY:	NTE 30 days a/o $500

STATUTE:	Disorderly Conduct 711–1101
OFFENSE:	Public display of offensive utterance or gesture intending to cause inconvenience, annoyance, or alarm.

---

[9]Decriminalized private consensual adult homosexual acts, 1972 Haw. Sess. Laws, Act 9, §1 (eff. Jan. 1, 1973).

STATUS: Violation
PENALTY: NTE $500

STATUTE: Open Lewdness
              712–1217
OFFENSE: Commission of any lewd act in a public place
              under circumstances likely to cause affront or
              alarm. (No further statutory explanation given.)
STATUS: Petty misd.
PENALTY: NTE 30 days a/o $500

IDAHO

STATUTE: Public Display of Offensive Sexual Material
              18–4105
OFFENSE: Exhibition or display in public of genitals or
              pubic area, or actual or simulated sex act.
STATUS: Misd.
PENALTY: NTE 6 mos. a/o $300

STATUTE: Crime Against Nature
              18–6605
OFFENSE: Performance of sodomy, fellatio, or any other
              unnatural copulation.
STATUS: Felony
PENALTY: NLT 5 yrs.

ILLINOIS[10]

STATUTE: Public Indecency
              38–11–9
OFFENSE: Performance of anal or oral sex, lewd exposure
              of one's body for sexual arousal, or lewd fon-
              dling or caressing of another person's body in a
              public place.
STATUS: Class A misd.
PENALTY: NTE 1 yr. a/o $1,000

[10]Decriminalized private consensual adult homosexual acts, 1961 Ill. Laws,
p. 1983, §11–2 (eff. Jan. 1, 1962).

INDIANA[11]

STATUTE: Definition of Deviate Sexual Conduct
           35–41–1–2
OFFENSE: Any act of sexual gratification involving the mouth
           or anus of one person, and the sex organs of
           another.

STATUTE: Public Indecency
           35–45–4–1
OFFENSE: Intentional performance of sexual intercourse or
           deviate sexual intercourse, or nudity, or fondling
           one's own genitals, or those of another in a
           public place.
STATUS: Class A misd.
PENALTY: NTE 1 yr. a/o $5000

IOWA[12]

STATUTE: Indecent Exposure
           709.9
OFFENSE: Exposure of genitals or pubes to another per-
           son, or commission of a sex act in front of an-
           other person knowing that the act is offensive to
           the viewer.
STATUS: Serious misd.
PENALTY: NTE 1 yr. a/o $1,000

KANSAS

STATUTE: Sodomy
           21–3505
OFFENSE: Oral or anal copulation between persons who are
           not husband and wife or consenting adult mem-
           bers of the opposite sex.
STATUS: Class B misd.
PENALTY: NTE 6 mos. a/o $1,000

[11]Decriminalized private consensual adult homosexual acts, 1976 Ind.
Act, P.L. 148, §24 (eff. July 1, 1977).
[12]Decriminalized private consensual adult homosexual acts, 1976 Ia. Acts,
ch. 1245, §520 (eff. Jan. 1, 1978).

STATUTE: Lewd & Lascivious Behavior
             21–3508
OFFENSE: Commission of any sex act with reasonable anticipation of being viewed by others, or exposure of one's sex organs for sexual arousal to another who has not consented.
STATUS: Class B misd.
PENALTY: NTE 6 mos. a/o $1,000

STATUTE: Disorderly Conduct
             21–4101
OFFENSE: Using offensive, obscene, or abusive language likely to arouse alarm, anger, or resentment in others.
STATUS: Class C misd.
PENALTY: NTE 1 mo. a/o $500

STATUTE: Vagrancy
             21–4108
OFFENSE: Loitering on the streets or in a public place intending to solicit someone for immoral purposes. (No further statutory explanation given.)
STATUS: Class C misd.
PENALTY: NTE 1 mo. a/o $500

KENTUCKY

STATUTE: Definition of Deviate Sexual Intercourse
             510.010
OFFENSE: Any act of sexual gratification involving the sex organs of one person, and the mouth or anus of another between persons not married to each other.

STATUTE: Sodomy
             510.100
OFFENSE: Engaging in deviate sexual intercourse with a person of the same sex. Consent is no defense.
STATUS: Class A misd.
PENALTY: NTE 1 yr. a/o $500

STATUTE: Indecent Exposure
             510.150
OFFENSE: Intentional exposure of one's genitals under cir-
             cumstances likely to cause affront or alarm.
STATUS: Class B misd.
PENALTY: NTE 90 days a/o $250

STATUTE: Harassment
             525.070
OFFENSE: Making an offensively coarse utterance, gesture,
             or display, or addressing abusive language to
             another person in a public place.[13]
STATUS: Violation
PENALTY: NTE $250

LOUISIANA

STATUTE: Crime Against Nature
             14.89
OFFENSE: Any sex act involving the mouth or anus of one
             person, and the sex organs of another.
STATUS: Felony
PENALTY: NTE 5 yrs. a/o $2,000

STATUTE: Disturbing the Peace
             14.103
OFFENSE: Addressing any offensive, derisive, or annoying
             words to another person in public, or calling
             anyone an offensive or derisive name.
STATUS: Misd.
PENALTY: NTE 90 days a/o $100

STATUTE: Obscenity
             14.106
OFFENSE: Public exposure of genitals, pubic hair, anus,
             vulva, or female breast to arouse sexual desire,
             or in a way which appeals to prurient interests,
             or is patently offensive.

[13]Held unconstitutional for overbreadth United States v Sturgill, 563
F.2d 307 (6th Cir. 1977).

STATUS: Misd.
PENALTY: NLT 6 mos., NTE 3 yrs. a/o NLT $1,000, NTE $2,500

MAINE[14]

STATUTE: Public Indecency
17–A–854
OFFENSE: Engaging in any sex act or exposing one's genitals causing affront or alarm, in a public place or in a private place which may be viewed from a public place, or another private place.
STATUS: Class E crime
PENALTY: NTE $500

MARYLAND

STATUTE: Lewdness
27–15
OFFENSE: Engaging in, permitting others to engage in, or soliciting any unnatural sexual practice.
STATUS: Misd.
PENALTY: NTE 1 yr. a/o $500

STATUTE: Disturbing the Peace
27–122
OFFENSE: Using obscene language or profanely cursing in a public place.
STATUS: Misd.
PENALTY: NTE 30 days a/o $100

STATUTE: Sodomy
27–553
OFFENSE: Sodomy. (No further statutory explanation given.)
STATUS: Felony
PENALTY: NTE 10 yrs.

STATUTE: Unnatural or Perverted Sexual Practices
27–554

[14]Decriminalized private consensual adult homosexual acts, 1975 Me. Acts, ch. 499,§5 (eff. May 1, 1976).

OFFENSE: Commission of oral or any other unnatural sex act. Consent is no defense. (No further statutory explanation given.)
STATUS: Felony
PENALTY: NTE 10 yrs. a/o $1,000

MASSACHUSETTS

STATUTE: Open & Gross Lewdness
272–16
OFFENSE: Open and gross lewdness and lascivious behavior. (No further statutory explanation given.)[15]
STATUS: Felony
PENALTY: NTE 3 yrs. a/o $300

STATUTE: Resorting to Restaurant or Taverns for Immoral Purposes
272–26
OFFENSE: Entering a restaurant or bar for the purpose of soliciting another to engage in immoral conduct, or, as an owner, permitting others to do so. (No further statutory definition provided.)
STATUS: Misd.
PENALTY: NLT $25, NTE $500 a/o NTE 1 yr.

STATUTE: Sodomy & Buggery
272–34
OFFENSE: Anal Intercourse.
STATUS: Felony
PENALTY: NTE 20 yrs.

STATUTE: Unnatural & Lascivious Acts
272–35
OFFENSE: Performance of any sex act in deviation with accepted customs and manners.[16]
STATUS: Felony
PENALTY: NTE 5 yrs. a/o NLT $100, NTE $1,000

[15]Held unconstitutionally vague and overbroad. Revere v. Aucella, 369 Mass. 138, 338 N.E.2d 816, *appeal dismissed*, 429 U.S. 877 (1975).
[16]Held not applicable to private, consensual adult behavior. Commonwealth v. Balthazar, 318 N.E. 2d 478, 366 Mass. 298 (1974).

STATUTE: Disorderly Conduct
272–53
OFFENSE: Lewd, wanton, or lascivious behavior or speech in public, or exposure of one's genitals to another person.[17]
STATUS: Misd.
PENALTY: NTE 6 mos. a/o $200

MICHIGAN

STATUTE: Crime Against Nature
750.158
OFFENSE: Sodomy performed by a man with another man, woman, or animal.
STATUS: Felony
PENALTY: NTE 15 yrs.

STATUTE: Disorderly Persons
750.167
OFFENSE: Engaging in indecent or obscene conduct in a public place.
STATUS: Misd.
PENALTY: NTE 90 days a/o $100

STATUTE: Gross Lewdness
750.335
OFFENSE: Open and gross lewdness and lascivious behavior. (No further statutory definition given.)
STATUS: Misd.
PENALTY: NTE 1 yr. a/o $500

STATUTE: Indecent Exposure
750.335a
OFFENSE: Open and knowing exposure of one's body. (No further statutory explanation given.)
STATUS: Misd.
PENALTY: NTE 1 yr. a/o $500

STATUTE: Gross Indecency
750.338 & 750.338a

[17]Probhibition on "lewd, wanton, or lascivious" behavior held unconstitutionally vague. Commonwealth v. Sefranka, 414 N.E.2d 602 (1980).

STATUS: Felony
PENALTY: NTE 5 yrs a/o $2,500

STATUTE: Soliciting
             750.448
OFFENSE: Accosting, soliciting, or inviting another person
             in public, to do lewd or immoral act. (No fur-
             ther statutory explanation given.)
STATUS: Misd.
PENALTY: NTE 90 days a/o $100

MINNESOTA

STATUTE: Sodomy
             609.293
OFFENSE: Carnally knowing any person, with their con-
             sent, by the anus or mouth.
STATUS: Misd.
PENALTY: NTE 1 yr. a/o $1,000

STATUTE: Disorderly Conduct
             609.72
OFFENSE: Using offensive, obscene, or abusive language or
             boisterous and noisy conduct tending reasonably
             to arouse alarm, anger, or resentment in others.[18]
STATUS: Misd.
PENALTY: NTE 90 days a/o $100

STATUTE: Indecent Exposure
             617.23
OFFENSE: Public exposure of one's genitals, or public gross
             lewdness or lascivious behavior.
STATUS: Misd.
PENALTY: NTE 10 days a/o $5

MISSISSIPPI

STATUTE: Indecent Exposure
             97–29–31

---

[18]Provision relating to "offensive, obscene, or abusive language" held
limited to "fighting words." Matter of S.L.J., 263 N.W.2d 412 (1978).

OFFENSE: Exposure of one's genitals in a public place.
STATUS: Misd.
PENALTY: NTE 6 mos. a/o $500

STATUTE: Unnatural Intercourse
97–29–59
OFFENSE: Sodomy.
STATUS: Felony
PENALTY: NTE 10 yrs.

STATUTE: Disorderly Conduct
9753–3
OFFENSE: Making rude or obscene remarks or gestures, using profane language, or making indecent proposals to another person.
STATUS: Misd.
PENALTY: NTE 4 mos. a/o $200

STATUTE: Disturbance of Public Peace
97–35–15
OFFENSE: Disturbing others by profane, indecent, or offensive language or conduct.
STATUS: Misd.
PENALTY: NTE 6 mos. a/o $500

STATUTE: Vagrancy
97–35–39
OFFENSE: Leading an idle, immoral, or profligate life when one has no visible means of support, and is able to work, but does not do so.
STATUS: Misd.
PENALTY: NLT 10 days, NTE 30 days, or bond A/LT $201

MISSOURI

STATUTE: Definition of Deviate Sexual Intercourse
566.010
OFFENSE: Any sex act involving the genitals of one person, and the mouth, tongue, hand, or anus of another.

STATUTE: Sexual Misconduct
566.090

OFFENSE: Deviate sexual intercourse with another person of the same sex.
STATUS: Class A misd.
PENALTY: NTE 1 yr. a/o $1,000

STATUTE: Indecent Exposure
566.130
OFFENSE: Exposure of one's genitals under circumstances likely to cause affront or alarm.
STATUS: Class A misd.
PENALTY: NTE 1 yr. a/o $1,000

MONTANA

STATUTE: Indecent Exposure
45–5–504
OFFENSE: Exposure of one's genitals for sexual arousal under circumstances likely to cause affront or alarm.
STATUS: Misd.
PENALTY: NTE 6 mos. a/o $500

STATUTE: Deviate Sexual Conduct
45–5–505
OFFENSE: Sexual conduct or sexual intercourse between two persons of the same sex.
STATUS: Felony
PENALTY: NTE 10 yrs. a/o $50,000

NEBRASKA[19]

STATUTE: Public Indecency
28–806
OFFENSE: Performance of any sex act, exposure of one's genitals intending to cause affront of alarm, or lewd fondling or caressing of another person's body in public.
STATUS: Class II misd.
PENALTY: NTE 6 mos. a/o $1,000

[19]Decriminalized private consensual adult homosexual acts, 1977 Neb. Laws, L.B. 38, §328 (eff. July 1, 1978).

NEVADA

STATUTE:	Crime Against Nature 201.190
OFFENSE:	Anal intercouse, cunnilingus, or fellatio between consenting adults of the same sex.
STATUS:	Felony
PENALTY:	NLT 1 yr., NTE 6 yrs.

STATUTE:	Open or Gross Lewdness 201.210
OFFENSE:	Committing an act of open or gross lewdness. (No further statutory explanation given.)
STATUS:	Gross misd.
PENALTY:	NTE 1 yr. a/o $1,000

STATUTE:	Indecent or Obscene Exposure 201.220
OFFENSE:	Open and indecent or obscene exposure of one's person.
STATUS:	Gross misd.
PENALTY:	NTE 1 yr. a/o $1,000*

STATUTE:	Vagrancy 207.030
OFFENSE:	Soliciting anyone to engage in public lewd or dissolute conduct in a public place or loitering around, or engaging in, toilet to solicit any lewd, lascivious, or unlawful conduct.
STATUS:	Misd.
PENALTY:	NTE 6 mos. a/o $500

STATUTE:	Sex Offender Registration 207.151–201.157
OFFENSE:	Anyone who commits any sexual assault, rape, open or gross lewdness, or indecent exposure, must register with the county sheriff or Chief of Police within forty-eight hours of his or her arrival in the county.
STATUS:	Misd.
PENALTY:	NTE 6 mos. a/o $500

NEW HAMPSHIRE[20]

STATUTE: Disorderly Conduct
            644:2
OFFENSE: Using abusive or obscene language or making
            obscene gestures in public causing annoyance
            or alarm.
STATUS: Violation
PENALTY: NTE 1 yr. a/o $100

STATUTE: Indecent Exposure & Lewdness
            645:1
OFFENSE: Performing any sex act, exposing one's genitals,
            or performing any act of gross lewdness under
            circumstances likely to cause affront or alarm.
STATUS: Misd.
PENALTY: NTE 1 yr. a/o $1,000

NEW JERSEY[21]

STATUTE: Lewdness
            2C:14–4
OFFENSE: Exposure of one's genitals in public for sexual
            arousal under circumstances likely to cause af-
            front or alarm.
STATUS: Disorderly person offense
PENALTY: NTE 6 mos. a/o $1,000

STATUTE: Disorderly Conduct
            2C:33–2
OFFENSE: Using unreasonably loud and offensively coarse
            or abusive language in a public place intending
            to offend the hearer.
STATUS: Petty disorderly persons offense
PENALTY: NTE 30 days a/o $500

---

[20]Decriminalized private consensual adult homosexual acts, 1973 N.H.
Laws, §532:26 (eff. Nov. 1, 1973).
[21]Decriminalized private consensual adult homosexual acts, 1978 N.J.
Laws, c. 95, §2C:98–2 (eff. Sept. 1, 1979).

NEW MEXICO[22]

STATUTE: Indecent Exposure
30–9–14
OFFENSE: Intentional exposure of one's penis, testicles, vulva, or vagina to public view.
STATUS: Petty misd.
PENALTY: NTE 6 mos. a/o $500

STATUTE: Indecent Dancing
30–9–14.1
OFFENSE: Indecent exposure while dancing in a public place.
STATUS: Petty misd.
PENALTY: NTE 6 mos. a/o $500

STATUTE: Indecent Waitering
30–9–14.2
OFFENSE: Indecent exposure while serving food or beverages in a public place.
STATUS: Petty misd.
PENALTY: NTE 6 mos. a/o $500

STATUTE: Disorderly Conduct
30–20–1
OFFENSE: Indecent, profane, or disorderly conduct which tends to disrupt the peace. (No further statutory explanation given.)
STATUS: Petty misd.
PENALTY: NTE 6 mos. a/o $500

NEW YORK

STATUTE: Definition of Deviate Sexual Intercourse
130.00(2)
OFFENSE: Sexual conduct between persons not married to each other involving the mouth or anus of one person, and the sex organs of another.

[22]Decriminalized private consensual adult homosexual acts, 1975 N.M. Laws, ch. 109,§8 (eff. Jan. 1, 1976).

STATUTE: Consensual Sodomy
130.38

OFFENSE: Engaging in deviate sexual intercourse.[23]

STATUS: Class B misd.

PENALTY: NTE 3 mos. a/o $500

STATUTE: Disorderly Conduct
240.20

OFFENSE: Using abusive or obscene language or gestures in a public place causing inconvenience, annoyance, or alarm.

STATUS: Violation

PENALTY: NTE 15 days a/o $250

STATUTE: Harassment
240.25

OFFENSE: Using abusive or obscene language or gestures in a public place intending to harass, annoy, or alarm another person.

STATUS: Violation

PENALTY: NTE 15 days a/o $250

STATUTE: Loitering
240.35

OFFENSE: Remaining in a public place in order to engage in, or solicit, deviate sexual intercourse.

STATUS: Violation

PENALTY: NTE 15 days a/o $250

STATUTE: Lewdness
245.00

OFFENSE: Intentional exposure of genitals in a lewd manner or commission of any other lewd act in a public place.

STATUS: Class B misd.

PENALTY: NTE 3 mos. a/o $500

[23]Statute struck down as an unconstitutional infringement of the guarantees under the U.S. Constitution to privacy and to equal protection of the law. People v. Onofre, 51 N.Y. 2d 476, 434 N.Y.S. 2d 947, 415 N.E. 2d 936 (1980), *cert. denied*, 451 U.S. 987 (1981).

NORTH CAROLINA

STATUTE: Crime Against Nature
             14–177
OFFENSE: Anal or oral intercourse.
STATUS: Class H felony
PENALTY: NTE 10 yrs. a/o fine

STATUTE: Indecent Exposure
             14–190.9
OFFENSE: Willful exposure of private parts in public in
             the presence of a person of the opposite sex.
STATUS: Misd.
PENALTY: NTE 6 mos. a/o $500

STATUTE: Disorderly Conduct
             14–275.1
OFFENSE: Using vulgar, obscene, or profane language or
             engaging in disorderly conduct at any bus station,
             railroad station, or airport.
STATUS: Misd.
PENALTY: NTE 30 days a/o $50

NORTH DAKOTA[24]

STATUTE: Indecent Exposure
             12.1–20–12.1
OFFENSE: Exposing one's penis, vulva, or anus in a public
             place, intending to annoy or harass another per-
             son, or masturbating in a public place.
STATUS: Class B misd.
PENALTY: NTE 30 days a/o $500

STATUTE: Disorderly Conduct
             12.1–31–01
OFFENSE: Using abusive or obscene language or making
             an obscene gesture in a public place, or soliciting
             sexual conduct by loitering in a public place, in-
             tending to annoy, harass, or alarm another person.

[24]Decriminalized private consensual adult homosexual acts, 1977 N. D.
Sess. Laws, ch. 122, §1 (eff. Jan. 1, 1978).

STATUS: Class B misd.
PENALTY: NTE 30 days a/o $500

OHIO[25]

STATUTE: Importuning
             2907.07
OFFENSE: Soliciting a person of the same sex to engage in
             sexual activity knowing that such solicitation is
             offensive to the other person.[26]
STATUS: Misd. first degree
PENALTY: NTE 6 mos. a/o $1,000

STATUTE: Public Indecency
             2907.09
OFFENSE: Exposing one's genitals, masturbating, or engag-
             ing in sexual intercourse in a public place.
STATUS: Misd. fourth degree
PENALTY: NTE 30 days a/o $250

STATUTE: Disorderly Conduct
             2917.11
OFFENSE: Making an offensively coarse utterance, gesture,
             or display, or communicating grossly abusive
             language to any person.[27]
STATUS: Minor misd.
PENALTY: NTE $100

OKLAHOMA

STATUTE: Grossly Outraging Public Decency
             21–22
OFFENSE: Committing any act that openly outrages public
             decency or is injurious to public morals. (No
             further statutory explanation given.)

[25]Decriminalized private consensual adult homosexual acts, 1972 Ohio
Laws, 134 v. H 511, §2 (eff. Jan. 1, 1974).
[26]Construed to proscribe only "fighting words," words which by their
very utterance inflict injury or tend to incite any immediate breach of
the peace. State v. Phipps, 58 Ohio St. 2d 271, 389 N.E.2d 1128 (1979).
[27]Held limited to "fighting words." State v. Hoffman, 57 Ohio St. 2d
129, 387 N.E.2d 239 (1979).

STATUS: Misd.
PENALTY: NTE 1 yr. a/o $500

STATUTE: Crime Against Nature
           21–886
OFFENSE: Commission of any unnatural sex act, that is, sodomy, fellatio, or cunnilingus.
STATUS: Felony
PENALTY: NTE 10 years

STATUTE: Indecent Exposure
           21–1021
OFFENSE: Lewd exposure of one's genitals in any public place, or where others are present who would be offended.
STATUS: Felony.
PENALTY: NLT 30 days a/o $100; NTE 10 years a/o $10,000

STATUTE: Lewdness
           21–1029
OFFENSE: Soliciting or inducing another to commit an act of lewdness. (No further statutory explanation given.)
STATUS: Misd.
PENALTY: NLT 30 days, NTE 1 yr.

OREGON[28]

STATUTE: Accosting for Deviate Purposes
           163.455
OFFENSE: Inviting or requesting another person in a public place to engage in deviate sexual intercourse, that is, sodomy, fellatio, or cunnilingus.[29]
STATUS: Class C misd.
PENALTY: NTE 30 days a/o $500

STATUTE: Public Indecency
           163.465

[28]Decriminalized private consensual adult homosexual acts, 1971 Ore. Laws, ch. 743 §432 (eff. Jan. 1, 1972).
[29]Held unconsititional. State v. Tusek, 52 Or. App. 997, 630 P.2d 892 (1981).

OFFENSE: Exposing one's genitals, performing sexual intercourse, or performing deviate sexual intercourse in public.

STATUS: Class A misd.

PENALTY: NTE 1 yr. a/o $2,500

STATUTE: Disorderly Conduct
166.025

OFFENSE: Using obscene language or making an obscene gesture intending to cause public inconvenience, annoyance, or alarm.

STATUS: Class B misd.

PENALTY: NTE 6 mos. a/o $1,000

PENNSYLVANIA

STATUTE: Definition of Deviate Sexual Intercourse
18–3101

OFFENSE: Oral or anal intercourse between human beings who are not husband and wife.

STATUTE: Voluntary Deviate Sexual Intercourse
18–3124

OFFENSE: Engaging in deviate sexual intercourse voluntarily.[30]

STATUS: Misd. second degree

PENALTY: NTE 2 yrs. a/o $5,000

STATUTE: Indecent Exposure
18–3127

OFFENSE: Exposing one's genitals to anyone other than one's spouse, causing affront or alarm.

STATUS: Misd. second degree

PENALTY: NTE 2 yrs. a/o $5,000

STATUTE: Disorderly Conduct
18–5503

OFFENSE: Using obscene language or making an obscene gesture intending to cause public inconvenience, annoyance, or alarm.

[30]Held unconstitutional. Commonwealth v. Bonadio, 490 Pa. 91, 415 A.2d 47.

STATUS: Misd. third degree
PENALTY: NTE 1 yr. a/o $2,500

STATUTE: Lewdness
18–5901
OFFENSE: Performing a lewd act likely to be observed by others who would be affronted or alarmed.[31]
STATUS: Misd. third degree
PENALTY: NTE 1 yr. a/o $2,500

RHODE ISLAND

STATUTE: Crime Against Nature
11–10–1
OFFENSE: Engaging in any unnatural sex act, that is, fellatio, cunnilingus, or sodomy. Consent is no defense.
STATUS: Felony
PENALTY: NLT 7 yrs., NTE 20 yrs.

STATUTE: Loitering for Indecent Purposes
11–34–8
OFFENSE: Standing or wandering in a public place and attempting to engage passersby in conversation, or to stop motor vehicles, for the purpose of prostitution or any indecent act.
STATUS: Petty misd.
PENALTY: NTE 6 mos. a/o $500

STATUTE: Disorderly Conduct
11–45–1
OFFENSE: Exposing one's genitals in public to another person under circumstances likely to cause affront or alarm.
STATUS: Misd.
PENALTY: NTE 6 mos. a/o $500

SOUTH CAROLINA

STATUTE: Lewdness
16–15–90

---

[31]Held violative of the Fourteenth Amendment. Commonwealth v. Carbaugh, 17 Adams L. J. 176 (1976).

OFFENSE: Exposing indecently one's genitals for the purpose of prostitution or other indecency, or being in a place for the purpose of lewdness or prostitution.

STATUS: Misd.

PENALTY: NTE 30 days a/o $100

STATUTE: Buggery
16–15–120

OFFENSE: Sodomy

STATUS: Felony

PENALTY: NTE 5 yrs. a/o NLT $500

STATUTE: Indecent Exposure
16–15–130

OFFENSE: Willful and malicious indecent exposure of one's person in public. (No further statutory explanation given.)

STATUS: Misd.

PENALTY: Discretionary

SOUTH DAKOTA[32]

STATUTE: Indecent Exposure
22–24–1

OFFENSE: Intentionally exposing one's genitals in any place where there are persons to be offended or annoyed.

STATUS: Class 2 misd.

PENALTY: NTE 30 days a/o $100

TENNESSEE

STATUTE: Disturbing the Peace
39–1213

OFFENSE: Disturbing the peace by violent, profane, indecent, offensive, or boisterous conduct or language.

STATUS: Misd.

PENALTY: NLT $20, NTE $200 a/o NTE 30 days

[32]Decriminalized private consensual adult homosexual acts, 1976 S.D. Sess. Laws, ch. 158, §22–8 (eff. Apr. 1, 1977).

STATUTE:	Prostitution 39–3502
OFFENSE:	Engaging in sexual intercourse for hire or licentious sexual intercourse without hire. (No further statutory explanation given.)
STATUS:	Misd.
PENALTY:	NTE $50

STATUTE:	Crimes Againt Nature 39–3714
OFFENSE:	Engaging in sodomy, fellatio, or cunnilingus.
STATUS:	Felony
PENALTY:	NLT 5 yrs., NTE 15 yrs.

TEXAS

STATUTE:	Homosexual Conduct 21.06
OFFENSE:	Engaging in any sex act involving the genitals of one person, and the mouth or anus of another person.[33]
STATUS:	Class C misd.
PENALTY:	NTE $200

STATUTE:	Lewdness 21.07
OFFENSE:	Engaging in sexual intercourse, deviate sexual intercourse, or any sexual contact in a public place.
STATUS:	Class A misd.
PENALTY:	NTE 1 yr. a/o $2000

STATUTE:	Indecent Exposure 21.08
OFFENSE:	Exposing one's anus or genitals for sexual arousal in public.
STATUS:	Class C misd.
PENALTY:	NTE $200

---

[33]Declared unconstitutional as violating the guarantees of privacy and equal protection of the law. Baker v. Wade, 51 U.S.L.W. 2149 (N.D. Tex. Aug. 17, 1982).

STATUTE: Disorderly Conduct
             42.01
OFFENSE: Using abusive, indecent, profane, or vulgar lan-
             guage, or making an offensive gesture in public
             tending to incite an immediate breach of peace,
             or exposing one's anus or genitals in public.
STATUS: Class C misd.
PENALTY: NTE $200

UTAH

STATUTE: Sodomy
             76–5–403
OFFENSE: Engaging in any sexual act involving the geni-
             tals of one person, and the mouth or anus of
             another, regardless of the sex of either participant.
STATUS: Class B misd.
PENALTY: NTE 6 mos. a/o $299

STATUTE: Disorderly Conduct
             76–9–102
OFFENSE: Using abusive or obscene language, or making
             obscene gestures in public place causing in-
             convenience, annoyance, or alarm.
STATUS: Infraction
PENALTY: NTE 90 days a/o $299

STATUTE: Lewdness
             76–9–702
OFFENSE: Fornicating exposing one's genitals or performing
             any act of gross lewdness in a public place or under
             circumstances likely to cause affront or alarm.
STATUS: Class B misd.
PENALTY: NTE 6 mos. a/o $299

VERMONT[34]

STATUTE: Disorderly Conduct
             13–1026

[34]Decriminalized private consensual adult homosexual acts, 1977 Vt.
Acts, No. 51,§3 (eff. July 1, 1977).

OFFENSE: Using abusive or obscene language in a public place.
STATUS: Misd.
PENALTY: NTE 60 days a/o $500

STATUTE: Lewdness
            13–2601
OFFENSE: Open and gross lewd, and lascivious behavior. (No further statutory explanation given.)
STATUS: Felony
PENALTY: NTE 5 yrs a/o $300

STATUTE: Prostitution
            13–2632
OFFENSE: Engaging in prostitution or open and gross lewdness. (No further statutory explanation given.)
STATUS: Misd.
PENALTY: NTE 1 yr. or $100

VIRGINIA

STATUTE: Crimes Against Nature
            18.2–361
OFFENSE: Engaging in carnal behavior involving the mouth or anus of one person, and sex organs of another. Consent is no defense.[35]
STATUS: Class 6 felony
PENALTY: NLT 1 yr., NTE 5 yrs., or NTE 1 yr. a/o $1,000

STATUTE: Indecent Exposure
            18.2–387
OFFENSE: Displaying one's person or genitals obscenely in a public place.
STATUS: Class 1 misd.
PENALTY: NTE 1 yr. a/o $1,000

[35]Constitutionality upheld. Doe v. Commonwealth's Attorney, 403 F. Supp. 1199 (E.D. Va. 1975), *aff'd*, 425 U.S. 901 (1976).

164 *The Rights of Gay People*

WASHINGTON[36]

STATUTE:	Public Indecency 9A.88.010
OFFENSE:	Exposure of one's person in an obscene manner likely to cause affront or alarm.
STATUS:	Misd.
PENALTY:	NTE 90 days a/o $1,000

WEST VIRGINIA[37]

STATUTI :	Lewd & Lascivious Conduct 61–8–4
OFFENSE:	Open or gross lewdness or lasciviousness. (No further statutory explanation given.)
STATUS:	Misd.
PENALTY:	NLT $50, and NTE 6 mos. (term discretionary)

STATUTE:	Indecent Exposure 61–8B–10
OFFENSE:	Intentional exposure of one's sex organs or anus under circumstances likely to cause affront or alarm.
STATUS:	Misd.
PENALTY:	NTE 90 days or NTE $250 and 90 days

STATUTE:	Public Indecency 61–8B–11
OFFENSE:	Engaging in any overt act of sexual gratification or exposing one's genitals in public under circumstances likely to cause affront or alarm.
STATUS:	Misd.
PENALTY:	NTE $250

WISCONSIN

STATUTE:	Sexual Perversion 944.17

[36]Decriminalized private consensual adult homosexual acts, 1975 Wash. Laws, 1st exec. sess., ch. 260 (eff. July 1, 1976).
[37]Decriminalized private consensual adult homosexual acts, 1976 W. Va. Acts, ch. 43 (eff. June 1, 1976).

OFFENSE: Performing any act of sexual gratification involving the mouth or anus of one person, and the sex organs of another. Consent is no defense.
STATUS: Class A misd.
PENALTY: NTE 9 mos. a/o $10,000

STATUTE: Lewd & Lascivious Behavior
944.20
OFFENSE: Committing any act of sexual gratification knowing that others are present, or publicly exposing one's sex organs.
STATUS: Class A misd.
PENALTY: NTE 9 mos. a/o $10,000

STATUTE: Disorderly Conduct
947.01
OFFENSE: Engaging in indecent, profane, or disorderly conduct under circumstances likely to cause a disturbance.
STATUS: Class A misd.
PENALTY: NTE 9 mos. a/o $10,000

STATUTE: Vagrancy
947.02
OFFENSE: Soliciting another person in public, to commit a crime against sexual morality.
STATUS: Class C misd.
PENALTY: NTE 30 days a/o $500

WYOMING[38]

STATUTE: Prostitution
6–5–107
OFFENSE: Performing any act of sexual intercourse for hire, or indiscriminate sexual intercourse without hire.
STATUS: Misd.
PENALTY: NLT 4 mos., NTE 1 yr.

STATUTE: Public Indecency
6–5–301

[38]Decriminalized private consensual adult homosexual acts, 1977 Wyo. Sess. Laws, ch. 70, §3 (eff. May 27, 1977).

OFFENSE: Exposing one's genitals in public, or using any
             obscene or licentious gesture or words in the
             presence of a female.
STATUS: Misd.
PENALTY: NTE 3 mos. a/o $100

Appendix B

A Bibliography of Works on Law and Civil Rights of Interest to Gays*

Barnett, Walter. *Sexual Freedom and the Constitution*. University of New Mexico Press, 1973.

Baskett, Edward Eugene. *Entrapped: An Accused Homosexual Looks at American Justice*. Lawrence Hill & Co., 1976.

Blaine, William L. and John Bishop. *Practical Guide for the Unmarried Couple*. Two Continents/Sun River Press, 1976.

Community Attitudes on Homosexuality and About Homosexuals. A Report on the Environment in Norman, Oklahoma. Norman Human Rights Commission, 1978. ($2.50 prepaid from Norman Human Rights Commission, Box 370, Norman, OK 73070.)

Curry, F. Hayden and Denis Clifford. *A Legal Guide for Gay and Lesbian Couples*. Addison-Wesley, 1980.

DeBaugh, R. Adam. *Writing to Congress*. [Tips for contacting representatives in Congress.] (25¢ prepaid from Washington Field Office, Metropolitan Community Churches, 110 Maryland Ave. NE, Suite 201, DC 20002.)

*This list is part of *A Gay Bibliography*, 6th ed., 1980, published by the Gay Task Force of the American Library Association (Social Responsibilities Round Table). Other sections of the 16-page *A Gay Bibliography*, include "History and Biography," "Literature and the Arts," "Religion," "the Gay/Lesbian Movement," and "Human Sciences." *A Gay Bibliography* is available at $1 each for 1 or 2 copies, 85¢ each for 3 to 9 copies, and 70¢ each for 10 or more copies. (For costs outside the United States, please inquire.) Orders under $25 must be prepaid. Checks and money orders should be payable to "Barbara Gittings—GTF," and sent to Barbara Gittings, GTF Coordinator, P.O. Box 2383, Philadelphia, PA 19103.

Digest on Gay Rights I: Human/Civil Rights Legislation. [Background, lists of supporting groups, public opinion; both U.S. & Canada.] (Gays for Equality, Box 27 UMSU, University of Manitoba, Winnipeg, Man., Canada R3T 2N2; U.S. orders, 2 International Postal Reply Coupons; Canada orders, 50¢ postage.)

Dworkin, Ronald. "Liberty and Moralism." Chapter 10 in his: *Taking Rights Seriously*. Harvard University Press, 1977.

Final Report of the Task Force on Sexual Preference. State of Oregon, Dept. of Human Resources, December 1978. (Available from Holly Hart [chairperson of the Task Force], 6915 SW Florence, Portland, OR 97223; $4 prepaid book rate, $3 each additional copy; $6.50 prepaid first class.)

Gay Civil Rights Support Packet. [Statements from organizations in science, religion, law, health, government, etc.] ($2 prepaid from National Gay Task Force, 80 5th Ave., NYC 10011.)

A Gay Parents' Legal Guide to Child Custody. Anti-Sexism Committee, San Francisco-Bay Area National Lawyers Guild, 2nd ed., 1980. [How legal system works in custody matters; personal decisions such as coming out & dealing with spouse; how to choose a lawyer.] ($2.40 prepaid from National Lawyers Guild, 558 Capp St., SF 94110.)

Gay Parents' Support Packet. [Information on child custody problems & strategies; cases that have won: resources list; studies of children of gays, etc.] ($2.50 prepaid from National Gay Task Force, 80 5th Ave., NYC 10011.)

Gay Rights Protections in U.S. and Canada. [List of law changes, revised quarterly.] (National Gay Task Force, 80 5th Ave., NYC 10011; free for self-addressed envelope #10 size with U.S. postage or small coin donation to cover.)

Gay Rights Skills Seminar Manual: What Every Progressive Lawyer and Legal Worker Should Know About the Everyday Problems of Gay People. Gay Rights Task Force. National Lawyers Guild, 2nd ed., 1979. (National Lawyers Guild. 558 Capp St., SF 94110; $10 Guild members, $15 nonmembers, $20 institutions, all plus $1 p/h.)

Gay Teachers Support Packet. [Statements on rights of gay teachers, from professional groups, school boards, etc.] ($2 prepaid from National Gay Task Force, 80 5th Ave., NYC 10011.)

Gengle, Dean. "Szasz on Gay Rights, Psychiatry and Liberty." *The Illinois Libertarian*, December 1979. (Reprints $1 prepaid from Jim Peron, Box 2140, Glen Ellyn, IL 60137.)

Gibson, E. Lawrence. *Get Off My Ship! Ensign Berg vs. The U.S. Navy*. Avon, 1978.

Gibson, Clifford Guy with the collaboration of Mary Jo Risher. *By Her Own Admission: A Lesbian Mother's Fight To Keep Her Son*. Doubleday, 1977.

Hodgdon, Virginia et al., editors. 1980 *Gay Civil Rights Legislation in Massachusetts*. Massachusetts Gay Political Caucus, 1980. [Background information for legislators; support statements; etc.] ($1 prepaid from MGPC, 118 Mass. Ave. —Box 179, Boston, MA 02115.)

Jay, Eric. *Will My Support For Gay Civil Rights Cost Me My Political Career?* Gay Rights National Lobby and National Gay Task Force, 1980. [Study of consequences for legislators at all government levels who have supported gay rights.] ($3 prepaid from Gay Rights National Lobby, Box 1892. DC 20013.)

Knutson, Donald C. *Homosexuality and the Law*. Vol. 1 in monograph series "Research and Homosexuality." [Special hardbound double issue of *Journal of Homosexuality* 5, Nos. 1 & 2.] The Haworth Press, 1980.

The Law and the Homosexually-Oriented Person. [Of value only in Canada.] (Available free from Gays for Equality, Box 27 UMSU, University of Manitoba, Winnipeg, Man., Canada R3T 2N2.)

Legal Protections Against Sexual Orientation Discrimination, City of Seattle—Information Sheet. (Available for stamped reply envelope #10 size from Seattle Office of Women's Rights, 400 Yesler, 3rd floor, Seattle, WA 98104.)

A Legislative Guide to Gay Rights. Portland Town Council, 1976. [Deals with legislators' objections to gay rights laws; basic material on homosexuality including young gays & gays in education; legislative history; support statements.] ($5 prepaid, flawed copies $2.50, from Portland Town Council, 320 SW Stark, #506, Portland, OR 97204.)

Lesbian Rights Handbook. Lesbian Rights Project, 1980 (June). [Employment, wills, shared property, crisis issues, housing, rights of young lesbians, lesbian businesses, etc.] (Lesbian Rights Project, 1370 Mission St., SF 94103.)

O'Leary, Jean and Bruce Voeller, "Gay Rights Law: Confusion En Route to Equality." [Overview of gay rights in non-legal language.] *Juris Doctor* 8 (June–July 1978): starts p. 36.

Pennsylvania Council for Sexual Minorities, Annual Reports. First Annual Report, March 1977; Second Annual Report, March 1978. (Available free from Penna. Council for Sexual Minorities, Rm. 238 Main Capitol Bldg., Harrisburg, PA 17120.)

Raico, Ralph. *Gay Rights: A Libertarian Approach*. The Libertarian Party, 1976. (50¢ prepaid from Libertarian Party, 2300 Wisconsin Ave. NW, DC 20007.)

Sexual Orientation Report. State of Michigan, Dept. of Civil Rights, 1977. (Available from Ruth Rasmussen, Director. Dept. of Civil Rights, Senate Office Building, 125 W. Allegan. Lansing, MI 48913; send 9 × 12 reply envelope with 53¢ postage.)

Sexual Preference Study. City of Tulsa, Dept. of Human Rights, 1976. (Dept. of Human Rights, Rm. 216, 200 Civic Center, Tulsa, OK 74103.)

"Symposium: Sexual Preference and Gender Identity." Issue of *Hastings Law Journal* 30, March 1979. ($3 prepaid from *Hastings Law Journal*, 198 McAllister St., SF 94102.)

Appendix C

Antidiscrimination Laws of Minneapolis, Minnesota, and East Lansing, Michigan

Minneapolis, Minnesota

AN ORDINANCE

Amending Chap 945 of the Minneapolis Code of Ordinances relating to Civil Rights. (99–68)
The City Council of the City of Minneapolis do ordain as follows:

SEC. 1. That subdivisions (a), and (b) of Sec 945.010 of the above entitled ordinance be amended to read as follows:
945.010. Findings, Declaration of Policy and Purpose.
(a) Findings. It is determined that discriminatory practices based on race, color, creed, religion, national origin, sex OR AFFECTIONAL OR SEXUAL PREFERENCE, with respect to employment, labor union membership, housing accommodations, property rights, education, public accommodations, and public services, or any of them, tend to create and intensify conditions of poverty, ill health, unrest, civil disobedience, lawlessness, and vice and adversely affect the public health, safety, order, convenience, and general welfare; such discriminatory practices threaten the rights, privileges and opportunities OF ALL INHABITANTS OF THE CITY AND SUCH RIGHTS, PRIVILEGES AND OPPORTUNITIES are hereby declared to be civil rights, and the adoption of this Chapter is deemed

to be an exercise of the police power of the City to protect such rights.

(b) Declaration of Policy and Purpose. It is the public policy of the City of Minneapolis and the purpose of this Chapter:

(1) To declare as civil rights the rights of all persons to the fullest extent of their capacities, and without regard to race, color, creed, religion, ancestry, national origin, sex OR AFFECTIONAL OR SEXUAL PREFERENCE, equal opportunities with respect to employment, labor union membership, housing accommodations, property rights, education, public accommodations, and public services;

(2) To prevent and prohibit any and all discriminatory practices based on race, color, creed, religion, ancestry, national origin, sex, OR AFFECTIONAL OR SEXUAL PREFERENCE, with respect to employment, labor union membership, housing accommodations, property rights, education, public accommodations, or public services;

(3) To protect all persons from unfounded charges of discriminatory practices;

(4) To effectuate the foregoing policy by means of public information and education, mediation and conciliation, and enforcement; and

(5) To eliminate existing and the development of any new ghettos in the community.

SEC 2. That subdivisions (r) and (s) of Sec 945.020 of the above entitled ordinance be amended to read as follows:

945.020. Definitions.

(r) Discrimination. "Discrimination" means any act or attempted act which because of race, color, creed, religion, ancestry, national origin, sex, OR AFFECTIONAL OR SEXUAL PREFERENCE, results in the unequal treatment or separation or segregation of any person, or denies, prevents, limits, or otherwise adversely affects, or if accomplished would deny, prevent, limit, or otherwise adversely affect, the benefit of enjoyment by any person of employment, membership in a labor organization, ownership or occupancy of real property, a public accommodation, a public service, or an educational institution. Such discrimination is unlawful and is a violation of this ordinance.

(s) AFFECTIONAL OR SEXUAL PREFERENCE. "AFFECTIONAL OR SEXUAL PREFERENCE," MEANS

HAVING OR MANIFESTING AN EMOTIONAL OR PHYSICAL ATTACHMENT TO ANOTHER CONSENTING PERSON OR PERSONS, OR HAVING OR MANIFESTING A PREFERENCE FOR SUCH ATTACHMENT.

SEC 3. That Sec 945.030 of the above entitled ordinance be amended to read as follows:

945.030. Violations.

(a) Act of Discrimination. Without limitation, the following are declared to be discrimination:

(1) For an employer, because of race, color, creed, religion, ancestry, national origin, sex OR AFFECTIONAL OR SEXUAL PREFERENCE, to fail or refuse to hire; to discharge an employee; or to accord adverse, unlawful or unequal treatment to any person or employee with respect to application, hiring, training, apprenticeship, tenure, promotion, upgrading, compensation, layoff, discharge, or any term or condition of employment except when based on a bona fide occupational qualification.

(2) For an employment agency, because of race, color, creed, religion, ancestry, national origin, sex OR AFFECTIONAL OR SEXUAL PREFERENCE, to accord adverse, unlawful or unequal treatment to any person in connection with any application for employment, any referral, or any request for assistance in procurement of employees, or to accept any listing of employment on such a basis, except when based on a bona fide occupational qualification.

(3) For any labor organization, because of race, color, creed, religion, ancestry, national origin, sex OR AFFECTIONAL OR SEXUAL PREFERENCE, to deny full and equal membership rights to an applicant for membership or to a member; to expel, suspend or otherwise discipline a member; or to accord adverse, unlawful or unequal treatment to any person with respect to his hiring, apprenticeship, training, tenure, compensation, upgrading, layoff or any term or condition of employment, except when based on a bona fide occupational qualification.

(4) For any person, having any interest in real property and any real estate broker or real estate agent, because of race, color, creed, religion, ancestry, national origin, sex OR AFFECTIONAL OR SEXUAL PREFERENCE, to fail or refuse to sell, rent, assign, or otherwise transfer any real property to any other person, or to accord adverse,

unlawful, or unequal treatment to any person with respect to the acquisition, occupancy, use, and enjoyment of any real property.

(5) For any person engaged in the provision of public accommodations, because of race, color, creed, religion, ancestry, national origin, sex OR AFFECTIONAL OR SEXUAL PREFERENCE, to fail or refuse to provide to any person access to the use of and benefit from the services and facilities of such public accommodations; or to accord adverse, unlawful, or unequal treatment to any person with respect to the availability of such services and facilities, the price or other consideration therefor, the scope and quality thereof, or the terms and conditions under which the same are made available, including terms and conditions relating to credit, payment, warranties, delivery, installation, and repair.

(6) For any person engaged in the provision of public services, by reason of race, color, creed, religion, ancestry, national origin, sex OR AFFECTIONAL OR SEXUAL PREFERENCE, to fail or refuse to provide to any person access to the use of and benefit thereof, or to provide adverse, unlawful, or unequal treatment to any person in connection therewith.

(7) For any person, because of race, color, creed, religion, ancestry, national origin, sex OR AFFECTIONAL OR SEXUAL PREFERENCE, to conceal or attempt to conceal any unlawful discrimination or to aid, abet, compel, coerce, incite or induce, or attempt to induce, another person to discriminate, or by any means, trick artifice, advertisement or sign, or use any form of application, or make any record on inquiry, or device, whatsoever to bring about or facilitate discrimination, or to engage in or threaten to engage in any reprisal, economic or otherwise, against any person by reason of the latter's filing a complaint, testifying or assisting in the observance and support of the purposes and provisions of this Chapter.

(8) For any person, bank, banking organization, mortgage company, insurance company, or other financial institution or lender to whom application is made for financial assistance for the purchase, lease, acquisition, construction, rehabilitation, repair, or maintenance of any real property or any agent or employee thereof to discriminate

against any person or group of persons, because of race, color, creed, religion, ancestry, national origin, sex OR AFFECTIONAL OR SEXUAL PREFERENCE of such person or group of persons or of the prospective occupants or tenants of such real property in the granting, withholding, extending, modifying, renewing, or in the rates, terms, conditions or privileges of any such financial assistance or in the extension of services in connection therewith.

(9) Wherever religious organizations or bodies are exempt from any of the provisions of this ordinance such exemption shall apply only to religious qualifications for employment or residence in church owned or operated property, and such organizations shall not be exempt from any provisions of this Chapter relating to discrimination based upon race, color, ancestry, national origin, sex OR AFFECTIONAL OR SEXUAL PREFERENCE.

SEC 4. That subparagraph (1) of subdivision (d) of Sec 945.060 of the above entitled ordinance be amended to read as follows:

(d) Substantive and Procedural Power and Duties. The Commission shall:

(1) Seek to prevent and eliminate bias and discrimination because of race, color, creed, religion, ancestry, national origin, sex OR AFFECTIONAL OR SEXUAL PREFERENCE, by means of education, persuasion, conciliation, and enforcement, and utilize all of the powers at its disposal to carry into execution the provisions of this Chapter.

East Lansing, Michigan

ORDINANCE NO. 325

AN ORDINANCE TO AMEND SECTIONS 1.124, 1.126 AND 1.127 OF CHAPTER 4 OF TITLE 1 OF THE CODE OF THE CITY OF EAST LANSING.

The City of East Lansing Ordains:

Section 1. Section 1.124 of the Code of the City of East Lansing shall be amended to read:

Section 1.124. *Duties.* It shall be the duty of the Human Relations Commission to protect and to promote the concept of human dignity and respect for the rights of all individuals and groups within the community; and to promote amicable relations among all individuals and groups within the city; to assemble, analyze, and disseminate authentic and factual data relating to group and individual relationships.

It shall have the power to publish and distribute such factual material as it deems necessary or desirable and to make such investigations, studies, and surveys as are necessary for the performance of its duties. It shall also make such recommendations as it deems necessary to the City Council when adopted by an affirmative vote of six members of the Commission. The Commission shall annually report its activities to the City Council.

Section 2. Section 1.126 of the Code of the City of East Lansing shall be amended to read:

Section 1.126 *Public Policy*. It is hereby declared to be contrary to the public policy of the City of East Lansing for any person to deny any other person the enjoyment of his civil rights or for any person to discriminate against any other person in the exercise of civil rights because of religion, race, color, sex or national origin.

Section 3. Section 1.127 of the Code of the City of East Lansing shall be amended to read:

Section 1.127. *Civil Rights Defined*. Employment. The opportunity to obtain employment without discrimination because of race, color, sex, religion, or national origin is hereby recognized and declared to be a civil right. Further it shall be contrary to the public policy of the City of East Lansing for any employer, because of the age of any individual, or because of the sex of any individual, or because of the sexual beliefs or sexual orientation of any individual, to refuse to hire or otherwise discriminate against him or her with respect to hire, tenure, terms, conditions or privileges of employment unless such refusal to hire or discrimination is based on a bona fide occupational qualification.

Housing. The opportunity to purchase, lease, sell, hold, use and convey dwelling houses or dwelling units without discrimination solely because of race, color, religion, sex, or national origin is hereby recognized and declared to be a civil right.

Public Accommodations. The opportunity to enjoy full and

equal accommodations, advantages, facilities and privileges
of inns, hotels, motels, government housing, restaurants,
eating houses, barber shops, billiard parlors, stores, public
conveyances on land and water, theaters, motion picture
houses, public educational institutions, in all methods of
air transportation and all other places of public accommodation, amusement, and recreation, without discrimination
solely because of race, color, sex, sexual orientation, religion, or national origin is hereby recognized and declared
to be a civil right.

Interpretation. Nothing contained in this section shall
be construed to limit the powers, duties, or responsibilities of the Human Relations Commission nor shall anything in this section be deemed in any manner to restrict
the definition of civil rights to those herein defined.

Appendix D

Executive Orders of the Governors of California and Pennsylvania

Executive Order of the Governor of California Prohibiting Discrimination in State Employment on the Basis of Sexual Preference.

WHEREAS, Article I of the California Constitution guarantees the inalienable right of privacy for all people which must be vigorously enforced; and

WHEREAS, government must not single out sexual minorities for harassment or recognize sexual orientation as a basis for discrimination; and

WHEREAS, California must expand its investment in human capital by enlisting the talent of all members of society;

NOW, THEREFORE, I, Edmund G. Brown Jr., Governor of the State of California, by virtue of the power and authority vested in me by the Constitution and statutes of the State of California, do hereby issue this order to become effective immediately:

The agencies, departments, boards and commissions within the Executive Branch of state government under the jurisdiction of the Governor shall not discriminate in state employment against any individual based solely upon the individual's sexual preference. Any alleged acts of discrimination in violation of this directive shall be reported to the State Personnel Board for resolution.

IN WITNESS WHEREOF, I have
hereunto set my hand and
caused the Great Seal of
the State of California to
be affixed this 4th day of
April, 1979.

Edmund G. Brown Jr.
Governor of California

Executive Order of the Governor of Pennsylvania Establishing a Council for Sexual Minorities.

COMMITMENT TOWARD EQUAL RIGHTS

In furtherance of my commitment to provide leadership
in the effort to obtain equal rights for all persons in Pennsylvania, this administration is committed to work towards
ending discrimination against persons solely because of
their affectional or sexual preference.

ESTABLISHMENT OF A COUNCIL FOR SEXUAL MINORITIES

To further this commitment, there is hereby established
the Pennsylvania Council for Sexual Minorities.
1. Composition of Council.
    a. The Council for Sexual Minorities shall be com-
posed of not more than thirty-five members appointed by
the Governor as follows: one representative each from the
Departments of Justice, Health, Welfare, and Education,
the Pennsylvania State Police, the Office of Administration, the Pennsylvania Commission for Women, and the
Pennsylvania Human Relations Commission; and representatives of the general public.
    b. The Governor shall designate one member as Chair-
person of the Council.
    c. Members of the Council shall serve for terms of
one or two years as the Governor shall designate. The
Governor shall fill any vacancies which may occur.

d. Members of the Council from the general public shall serve without salary but shall be reimbursed for necessary expenses incurred while attending official Council meetings and performing other official functions as the Chairperson, with the written approval of the Governor's Office, shall prescribe.

2. Functions.

a. The Council shall study problems of sexual minorities and make recommendations to the Governor as to policy and legislative changes needed to further the goal of obtaining equal rights for all persons.

b. The Council shall work with state agencies to end discrimination against persons solely on the basis of their affectional or sexual preference.

c. The Council shall work to educate state personnel and the public in general about problems and issues affecting sexual minorities.

d. The Council is authorized to receive complaints from persons claiming that they have been discriminated against on the basis of sexual or affectional preference for the purpose of referring such complaints to an appropriate place for resolution, where possible.

e. The Council shall adopt rules of procedures consistent with the provisions of this Executive Order.

f. The Council shall convene for meetings or hearings at the call of its Chairperson. A majority of appointed members shall constitute a quorum for the purpose of conducting the business of the Council. A vote of the majority of members present shall be sufficient for all actions of the Council.

g. The Council shall issue an annual report to the Governor.

3. Duties of Agencies Under the Governor's Jurisdiction.

Agencies under the Governor's jurisdiction are hereby directed to cooperate with the Pennsylvania Council for Sexual Minorities and to supply the Council with information requested in order that goals of this Executive Order may be realized.

> (Signed by Milton J. Shapp,
> Governor, as amended,
> February 11, 1975)

Appendix E

A Selective List of Gay Organizations

There are now thousands of gay and lesbian-feminist organizations in the United States—far too many to list in this handbook. Here is a sampling of groups offering help or information to gays, and those interested in gay issues. They can, of course, direct you to other resources available near you.

The authors gratefully acknowledge the assistance of Tom Burrows, Larry Gurel, and the National Gay Task Force, in the preparation of this list.

National

American Civil Liberties Union
National Gay Rights Project
633 S. Shatto St., Suite 207
Los Angeles, CA 90048
(213) 487–1720

Gay & Lesbian Advocates & Defenders
2 Park Sq.
Boston, MA 02116
(617) 426–2020

Gay Rights Advocates
540 Castro St.
San Francisco, CA 94114
(415) 863–3622

Gay Rights National Lobby
P.O. Box 1892
Washington, DC 20013
(202) 546–1801

Lambda Legal Defense & Education Fund
132 W. 43 St.
New York, NY 10036
(212) 944–9488

Lesbian Mothers National
Defense Fund
2446 Lorentz Pl., N.
Seattle, WA 98109
(206) 282–5798
(206) 284–2290

National Association of
Business Councils
244 W. 49 St., Suite 200
New York, NY 10019

National Coalition of Black
Gays
P.O. Box 57236
West End Sta.
Washington, DC 20037
(202) 387–8096

National Educational
Foundation for Individual
Rights
c/o Lesbian Rights Project
1370 Mission St.
San Francisco, CA 94103
(415) 441–2629

National Federation of
Parents & Friends of Gays
5715 16th St. N.W.
Washington, DC 20011
(202) 726–3223

National Gay Task Force
80 Fifth Ave., Suite 1601
New York, NY 10011
(212) 741–5800

State & Local

Alabama

Lambda, Inc.
P.O. Box 73062
Birmingham, AL 35223

Gay Information Line:
(205) 251–0682

Alaska

Alaska Gay & Lesbian
Activists Alliance
Box 2553
Anchorage, AK 99510
(907) 272–0456

Arizona

Alternative Relations
Center
Box 23004, 1836 Grand Ave.
Phoenix, AZ 85063
(602) 257–0350

Arkansas

Arkansas Gay Rights,
Inc.
P.O. Box 3115
Little Rock, AR 72203
(501) 376–7397

California

Gay & Lesbian Community
Center
330 Grove St.
San Francisco, CA 94102
(415) 863–9000

Gay & Lesbian Community
Services Center
Box 38777, 1213 N.
Highland Ave.
Los Angeles, CA 90038
(213) 464–7400

Gay Referral Line
P.O. Box 6046
San Francisco, CA 94101
(415) 756–7954

Lesbian/Gay Community
Center
1447 30 St.
San Diego, CA 92012
(714) 232–7528

Colorado

Gay Community Center of
Colorado
P.O. Box 18467
Denver, CO 80218
(303) 831–6268

Connecticut

Greater Hartford Lesbian &
Gay Task Force
P.O. Box 3241, Central
Station
Hartford, CT 06103
(203) 249–7691

New Haven Gay
Switchboard
P.O. Box 72
New Haven, CT 06501
(203) 624–6869

District of Columbia

Gay Community Center
1469 Church St., NW
Washington, DC 20005
(202) 232–7103

Gay Hot Line: (202)
833–3234

Delaware

Gay Community of
Delaware
P.O. Box 366
Newark, DE 19711

Florida

Dade County Coalition for
Human Rights
901 N.E. 79 St., Rm. 20
Miami, FL 33138
(305) 652–8945

Florida Task Force
P.O. Box 10367
Tallahassee, FL 32302

Georgia

Atlanta Gay Center, Inc.
Box 13723
931 Ponce de Leon Ave.,
N.E.
Atlanta, GA 30306

Gay Help Line:
(404) 892–0661
(404) 876–5372

Hawaii

Sexual Identity Center
Box 3224
Honolulu, HI 96801
(808) 521–4551

Idaho

Northwest Gay People's
Alliance
P.O. Box 8758
Moscow, ID 83843
(208) 882–1208

Illinois

Gay Horizons, Inc.
P.O. Box 1319
Chicago, IL 60690
(312) 929–HELP

Illinois Gay & Lesbian Task
Force
P.O. Box 909
Chicago, IL 60690
(312) 975–0707

Indiana

Gay People's Union of
Indiana, Inc.
P.O. Box 1881
Indianapolis, IN 46206
(317) 283–6977

Gay/Lesbian Switchboard
(317) 546–9339

Iowa

Gay Coalition of Iowa
P.O. Box 1953
Des Moines, IA 50306
(515) 288–3085

Gay People's Union
Univ. of Iowa Memorial Union
Student Activities Center
Iowa City, IA 52242
(319) 353–7162

Kansas

Gay Services of Kansas
P.O. Box 0, Kansas Union
Univ. of Kansas
Lawrence, KS 66045
(913) 842–7505
(913) 864–3091

Kentucky

Lambda/Louisville
P.O. Box 8415
Louisville, KY 40208

Louisiana

Louisiana Gay Political
Action Caucus
P.O. Box 53075
New Orleans, LA 70153
(504) 523–3922
(504) 945–1586

Maine

Maine Gay Task Force
P.O. Box 4542
Portland, ME 04112
(207) 773–5530

Gay Hotline: (207)
780–4055

Maryland

Gay Community Center of
Baltimore
P.O. Box 74
241 W. Chase St.
Baltimore, MD 21203
(301) 837–5445
(301) 837–8888

Massachusetts

Lesbian & Gay Hotline
P.O. Box 2009
Boston, MA 02106
(617) 426–9371

Massachusetts Gay Political
Caucus
118 N. Massachusetts Ave.
Boston, MA 02115
(617) 471–8404

Michigan

Michigan Organization For
Human Rights
940 W. McNichols
Detroit, MI 48203
(313) 863–7255

Gay Hotline: (313)
577–3450

Minnesota

Gay Community Services
2855 Park Ave. S.
Minneapolis, MN 55407
(612) 827–2821

Minnesota Committee For
Gay & Lesbian Rights
P.O. Box 993, Main Post
Office
Minneapolis, MN 55440
(612) 871–7913

Mississippi

Mississippi Gay Alliance
P.O. Box 8342
Jackson, MS 39207
(601) 353–6447

Missouri

Gay Hotline
P.O. Box 4915
St. Louis, MO 63108
(314) 367–0084

Montana

Out in Montana
P.O. Box 8896
Missoula, MT 59807
(406) 728–6589
(406) 728–8758

Nebraska

Gay Awareness
Iowa/Nebraska
P.O. Box 715, Downtown
Sta.
Omaha, NB 68101
(402) 553–5900

Gay/Lesbian Rap Line:
(402) 346–1698

Nevada

Nevadans for Human Rights
P.O. Box 18401–19D
Las Vegas, NV 89114
(702) 384–0726

New Hampshire

New Hampshire Coalition
of Lesbians & Gay Men
P.O. Box 521
Concord, NH 03301

New Jersey

Gay Activist Alliance
1734 S. Hackensack
Hackensack, NJ 07606
(201) 343–6402

New Jersey Gay Coalition
Rutgers Univ., P.O. Box 2901
New Brunswick, NJ 08903
(201) 249–1620

New Mexico

Gay & Lesbian Community
Association of
Albuquerque
106 Girard Blvd., SE,
Rm. 114
Albuquerque, NM 87106
(505) 268–9240

New York

Gay Community Center
332 Hudson Ave.
Albany, NY 12210
(518) 462–6138

Gay Switchboard
110 E. 23 St.
New York, NY 10010
(212) 777–1800

Lesbian Feminist Liberation
243 W. 20 St.
New York, NY 10011
(212) 691–5460

North Carolina

Carolina Gay Association
P.O. Box 39, Carolina Union
Chapel Hill, NC 27514
(919) 929–4997

North Dakota

AWARE
6 E. Lynmar
Fargo, ND 58102
(701) 280–1498

Ohio

Gay Line Cincinnati
P.O. Box 19158
Cincinnati, OH 45219
(513) 241–0001

Gay Switchboard/Hotline
P.O. Box 6177
Cleveland, OH 44101
(216) 621–3380

PRO/Toledo
P.O. Box 4642, Old West
End Sta.
Toledo, OH 43620
(419) 243–9351

Oklahoma

Oklahomans for Human
Rights
P.O. Box 207
Oklahoma City, OK 73101
(405) 840–3664
(405) 524–8941

Oklahomans for Human Rights
P.O. Box 52729
Tulsa, OK 74152

Oregon

Eugene Citizens for Human
Rights
P.O. Box 402
Eugene, OR 97440
(503) 485–1075

Portland Town Council
408 S.W. Second Ave.,
Suite 408
Portland, OR 97204
(503) 227–2765

Pennsylvania

Gay Community Center of
Philadelphia
P.O. Box 15748, 326
Kator St.
Philadelphia, PA 19103
(215) 922–1623

Gay Hotline: (215) 928–1919

Gay Switchboard
P.O. Box 872
Harrisburg, PA 17108
(717) 234–0328

Persad Center
814 Highland Bldg.

1121 S. Highland Ave.
Pittsburgh, PA 15206
(412) 441–0857

Puerto Rico

Comunidad de Orgullo Gay
Apartado 5532
Puerta de Tierra
San Juan, PR 00906
(809) 767–7722

Rhode Island

Gay Community Services
44 Washington St., Rm. 307
Providence, RI 02903
(401) 751–3322

South Carolina

Lambda of Charleston
c/o Unitarian Church
P.O. Box 772
Charleston, SC 29402
(803) 577–2743

SAGA
P.O. Box 1273
Anderson, SC 29622
(803) 266–6711

South Dakota

Sioux Empire Gay Coalition
P.O. Box 220
Sioux Falls, SD 57101
(605) 332–4599

Tennessee

Gay Switchboard of Memphis
P.O. Box 3038
Memphis, TN 38103
(901) 726–4299

Tennessee Gay Coalition
for Human Rights
P.O. Box 24181
Nashville, TN 37212

Texas

Dallas Gay Alliance
P.O. Box 35011
Dallas, TX 75235
(214) 528–4233

Gayline: (214) 748–6790

Gay Community Services
Univ. Y, 2330 Guadalupe St.
Austin, TX 78705
(512) 477–6699

Gay Resource Services
P.O. Box 309, U.C.
Univ. of Houston
Houston, TX 77004
(713) 749–3489

Gay Switchboard of San
Antonio
1136 W. Woodlawn
San Antonio, TX 78201
(512) 733–7300

Utah

Gay Helpline: (801) 533–0927

Vermont

Southern Vermont Lesbians &
Gay Men
P.O. Box 1034
Brattleboro, VT 05301
(802) 254–8176

Virginia

Unitarian-Univeralist Gay
Community
739 Yarmouth St.
Norfolk, VA 23510
(804) 625–1130

Virginia Coalition for Lesbian
& Gay Rights
P.O. Box 5522
Richmond, VA 23220
(804) 775–1518

Washington

Dorian Group
526 Smith Tower
Seattle, WA 98104
(206) 682–6044

West Virginia

WEVA GAY
P.O. Box 3583
Charleston, WV 25335

Wisconsin

Gay Peoples' Union
1568 No. Farwell Ave.
Milwaukee, WI 53202
(414) 271–5273

The United
302 No. Brooks
Madison, WI 53703
(608) 255–8582

Wyoming

Tri-State Lambda, Inc.
P.O. Box 1542
Cheyenne, WY 82001

Appendix F

ACLU State Affiliates

ALABAMA

Alabama CLU
P.O. Box 447
Montgomery, AL 36101
(205) 262-0304

ALASKA

Alaska CLU
1247 8th Ave.
Anchorage, AK 99501
(907) 349-5543

ARIZONA

Arizona CLU
1433 N. First. St.
Phoenix, AZ 85004
(602) 254-3339

ARKANSAS

ACLU of Arkansas
P.O. Box 2832
Little Rock, AR 72203
(501) 374-2660

CALIFORNIA

ACLU of Northern California
1663 Mission St., 4th Floor
San Francisco, CA 94103
(415) 621-2488

ACLU of Southern California
633 S. Shatto Place
Los Angeles, CA 90005
(213) 487-1720

COLORADO

ACLU of Colorado
815 E. 22 Ave.
Denver, CO 80205
(303) 861-2258

CONNECTICUT

Connecticut CLU
22 Maple Ave.
Hartford, CT 06114
(203) 247-9823

DISTRICT OF COLUMBIA

ACLU of the National Capital Area
600 Pennsylvania Ave., SE
Suite 301
Washington, DC 20003
(202) 544–1076

DELAWARE

ACLU of Delaware
1707 Farmers Bank Bldg.
Wilmington, DE 19801
(302) 654–3966

FLORIDA

ACLU of Florida
7210 Red Rd., Rm. 208
So. Miami, FL 33143
(305) 666–2950

GEORGIA

ACLU of Georgia
88 Walton St., NW
Atlanta, GA 30303
(404) 523–5398

HAWAII

ACLU of Hawaii
217 S. King St., Suite 307
Honolulu, HI 96813
(808) 538–7336

ILLINOIS

ACLU of Illinois
2205 State St. Suite 816
Chicago, IL 60604
(312) 427–7330

INDIANA

Indiana CLU
445 North Pennsylvania St.
Suite 604
Indianapolis, IN 46204
(317) 635–4056

Calumet Chapter
P.O. Box 2521
Gary, IN 46403
(219) 938–0663

IOWA

Iowa CLU
102 E. Grand Ave.,
Suite G–100
Des Moines, IA 50309
(515) 243–3576

KANSAS

Kansas ACLU of
1335 S. Water St.
Wichita, KS 67213
(316) 264–2718

KENTUCKY

Kentucky CLU
3618 Lexington Rd.
Louisville, KY 40207
(502) 895–0279

LOUISIANA

ACLU of Louisiana
348 Baronne St. Suite 324
New Orleans, LA 70112
(504) 522–0617

MAINE

Maine CLU
97A Exchange St.
Portland, ME 04101
(207) 774–5444

MARYLAND

ACLU of Maryland
744 Dulaney Valley Ct.
Suite 4
Towson, MD 21204
(301) 337-9233

MASSACHUSETTS

ACLU of Massachusetts
47 Winter St.
Boston, MA 02108
(617) 482–3170

MICHIGAN

ACLU of Michigan
110 Woodward Tower at the
Park
10 Witherell
Detroit, MI 48226
(313) 961–4662

MINNESOTA

Minnesota CLU
628 Central Ave.
Minneapolis, MN 55414
(612) 378–9392

MISSISSIPPI

ACLU of Mississippi
528 N. State St.
Jackson, MS 39201
(601) 582–2784

MISSOURI

ACLU of Eastern Missouri
5756 W. Park Ave.
St. Louis, MO 63110
(314) 647–4554

ACLU of Western Missouri
1627 Main, Suite 1210
Kansas City, MO 64108
(816) 421–1875

MONTANA

ACLU of Montana
P.O. Box 3012
Billings, MT 59103
(406) 248–1086

NEBRASKA

Nebraska CLU
511 Anderson Bldg.
P.O. Box 81455
Lincoln, NB 68501
(402) 476–8091

NEVADA

ACLU of Nevada
P.O. Box 9145
Reno, NV 89507

NEW HAMPSHIRE

New Hampshire CLU
11 S. Main
Concord, NH 03301
(603) 225–3080

NEW JERSEY

ACLU of New Jersey
38 Walnut St.
Newark, NJ 07102
(201) 642–2084

NEW MEXICO

ACLU of New Mexico
1330 San Pedro Dr., NE
Rm. 110
Albuquerque, NM 87110
(505) 266–5915

NEW YORK

New York CLU
84 Fifth Ave., Suite 300
New York, NY 10011
(212) 924–7800

NORTH CAROLINA

North Carolina CLU
P.O. Box 3094
Greensboro, NC 27402
(919) 273–1641

OHIO

ACLU of Ohio
360 S. 3rd St.
Suite 150
Columbus, OH 43215
(614) 228–8951

Greater Cleveland Chapter
1223 W. 6th St., 2nd Floor
Cleveland, OH 44113
(216) 781–6276

OKLAHOMA

ACLU of Oklahoma
P.O. Box 799
Oklahoma City, OK 73101
(405) 524–8511

OREGON

ACLU of Oregon
601 Willamette Bldg.
534 S.W. 3rd Ave.
Portland, OR 97204
(503) 227–3186

PENNSYLVANIA

ACLU of Pennsylvania
Juniper Bldg.
1324 Walnut St.
Philadelphia, PA 19107
(215) 735–7103

Pittsburgh Chapter
237 Oakland Ave.
Pittsburgh, PA 15213
(412) 681–7736

RHODE ISLAND

Rhode Island CLU
212 Union St. Rm. 408
Providence, RI 02903
(401) 831–7171

SOUTH CAROLINA

ACLU of South Carolina
533–B Harden St.
Columbia, SC 29205
(803) 799–5151

TENNESSEE

ACLU of Tennessee
81 Madison Bldg.
Suite 1501
Memphis, TN 38103
(901) 521–9875

TEXAS

Texas CLU
600 W. 7th St.
Austin, TX 78701
(512) 477–5849

Houston Chapter
1236 W. Gray
Houston, TX 77019
(713) 524–5925

UTAH

ACLU of Utah
632 Judge Bldg.
8 E. Broadway
Salt Lake City, UT 84111
(801) 521–9289

VERMONT

Vermont CLU
43 State St.
Montpelier, VT 05602
(802) 229–4900

VIRGINIA

ACLU of Virginia
112A N. 7th St.
Richmond, VA 23219
(804) 644–8022

WASHINGTON

ACLU of Washington
2101 Smith Tower
Seattle, WA 98104
(206) 624–2180

WEST VIRGINIA

West Virginia CLU
1105 Quarrier St.
Charleston, WV 25301
(304) 342-5318

WISCONSIN

Wisconsin CLU
783 N. Water St.
Suite 500
Milwaukee, WI 53202
(414) 272–4032

National Chapters

IDAHO

Boise Valley Natl. Chapter,
ACLU
P.O. Box 968
Boise, ID 83701

Southeast Idaho Natl. Chapter
2810 Holly Place
Idaho Falls, ID 83401

NORTH DAKOTA

Ward County (Minot)
National Chapter, ACLU
c/o Carl Kavelage
Political Science Division
Minot State College
Minot, ND 58701
(701) 838–6101

Red River Valley Natl. Chapter, ACLU
P.O. Box 5502
University Sta.
Fargo, ND 58105

SOUTH DAKOTA

South Dakota Natl. Chapter,
ACLU
P.O. Box 95
Sioux Falls, SD 57101

WYOMING

Laramie Natl. Chapter ACLU
2132 Rainbow
Laramie, WY 82070
(307) 745–3729

Regional Offices

Washington Office
600 Pennsylvania Ave., SE
Washington, DC 20003
(202) 544–1681

Southern Regional Office
52 Fairlie St., NW
Atlanta, GA 30303
(404) 523–2721

Mountain States
Regional Office
2160 S. Holly, Suite 201
Denver, CO 80222
(303) 753–1214